Teaching for Mastery in Writing

By Mike Cain

BLOOMSBURY EDUCATION
LONDON OXFORD NEW YORK NEW DELHI SYDNEY

BLOOMSBURY EDUCATION
Bloomsbury Publishing Plc
50 Bedford Square, London, WC1B 3DP, UK

BLOOMSBURY, BLOOMSBURY EDUCATION and the Diana logo are trademarks of
Bloomsbury Publishing Plc

First published in Great Britain, 2018

A catalogue record for this book is available from the British Library

ISBN: PB: 978-1-4729-4989-9;
ePDF: 978-1-4729-4988-2; ePub: 978-1-4729-4986-8

2 4 6 8 10 9 7 5 3

Typeset by Newgen KnowledgeWorks Pvt. Ltd., Chennai, India
Printed and bound in the UK by CPI Group (UK) Ltd, Croydon CR0 4YY

All papers used by Bloomsbury Publishing Plc are natural, recyclable products from wood grown
in well managed forests. The manufacturing processes conform to the environmental regulations of
the country of origin.

To find out more about our authors and books visit www.bloomsbury.com
and sign up for our newsletters.

Contents

Acknowledgements

I am hugely indebted to Frank Cottrell-Boyce for his inspirational foreword to this book. My sincere thanks also to the schools I worked with to trial some of the teaching strategies shared, and to the teachers who contributed case studies: Helen Cain and Sharon Houghton (St Thomas of Canterbury Catholic Primary), Rachel Draper and Rachael Szaloky (Sacred Heart Catholic Primary), Rebecca Taylor (St William's Catholic Primary), Janet Dean (Platt Bridge Community Primary), Sarah Platt (Queens Park Primary) and Ashley Riley (Moorfield Primary). I am grateful to my colleagues across the field of primary education who responded to my initial survey on maximising progress in writing. To Rory Orlandi for his unwavering belief in me and to Kathy Hall for giving me the freedom to develop the English curriculum at my own school. My family and friends have, as always, given me tremendous support. A special thank you to Alison and Allan for their encouragement, to Helen, Ella and Lydia for giving me the space and time I needed to work on the book and, finally, to Kathleen and Walter – for everything.

Foreword by Frank Cottrell-Boyce

I remember the day that I discovered the power of words. I was in Year 6. My best friend had been off school sick for some time and for some reason I opted to put the energy I usually put into distracting him at the back of the class into the piece of work I was doing. At the end of the lesson my teacher – a nun called Sister Paul – collected the work. She could see at a glance that I'd done something I didn't normally do. When she got to the front of the class, she turned around and read my piece out. Hearing my own words come back at me, over the heads of my peers, hearing them laugh in all the right places, was transformative. I could feel the definition of myself crystallising. It struck me for the first time that words didn't just come out of your mouth. You could choose them. If you chose the right one, you'd get a laugh. If you chose one that was both right and unexpected, you'd get an even bigger laugh. I realised that words were something that you could be good at – like football or maths. It's a moment I go back to all the time. To this day, if I have to watch a film I've written – at a festival or whatever – I will always sit at the back and part of me will be in Sr. Paul's class tingling with the excitement of discovery.

Mike Cain's ideas in this book are all about trying to create the conditions under which moments like this can happen, and to offer a strategy for learning to be good at words. Because just as with football and maths you can only get good at words if you practise, play, share, experiment and above all enjoy that richest of educational opportunities – failure.

Another anecdote. I took my daughter to Seven Stories – the wonderful museum of children's literature in Newcastle. Browsing their display of original manuscripts, she shouted 'Dad look at this! The Borrowers was rubbish!'. You need to know that she loved the Borrowers. But there was the original, finished manuscript all neatly typed with a terrible title 'Under the Floorboards' and the beloved characters with unenchanting picture book names I can't even bear to type. Mary Norton had crossed these out and, presumably at the very last minute, written over them in ink 'The Borrowers, Arietty, and Pod'.

By and large children's experience of writing in school is an experience of conformity – of getting things marked right, or marked wrong, of learning to make accurate notes or reproduce exam-friendly phrases or – God help us – using fronted adverbials or wow words. Obviously some of this (not the fronted adverbials) is a necessary part of the educational process but it's the opposite of writing. Learning to write is not about fitting your thoughts to a template. It's about finding your own voice. It's about learning to be. This is why learning to write is important.

For me, this is not about 'creative writing'. Against all the predictions of futurologists our children live in a written world. Verbal communication takes second place to tweets, messages, likes, and comments. It's part of a storm of verbiage that is characterised by anger and tribalism. Why is there so much fury online? Because expressing yourself is very difficult – you have to get good at it. And when it's difficult, the default is fury and name-calling. Nowadays fury and name-calling win elections. They are changing the shape of the world. It's more important than ever that our children get good at words.

Every year, for the last few years, I have been one of the judges of Radio 2's hugely popular 500 Words short story writing competition. It receives close to 200,000 entries and every year I and the other judges are astounded at the way the children have used the writing as an opportunity to engage with the joys and terrors of their own reality. Their world is full of digital distraction but the business of writing – what Frank O'Connor called 'the happiness of getting it down right' – makes them engage with the reality of where they live and who they are. At our last meeting we were given a moving letter from the mother of an autistic boy who was finding school so difficult he had stopped going but he'd decided to write something for the competition. Just five hundred words. He spent happy hours discussing it with his mother, writing and rewriting. In the end he was so happy with it he decided not to send it in but to frame it and put it on the wall. The journey through skills and trial and error leads into the secret chambers of the heart. Rilke once said that if you thought your life was boring it was because you were not enough of a poet to wake its soul. In teaching our children to write we are teaching them to wake up the soul of their world.

Frank Cottrell-Boyce is a British screenwriter, author and writer of the Olympic opening ceremony. He has won several awards for his screenplays, and lives in Liverpool with his family. His third novel, Cosmic, *was published in 2008, and was shortlisted for the Guardian Children's Fiction Prize and the Roald Dahl Funny Prize in the same year.*

Introduction: Mastery learning

Pretty much everyone can become an outstanding writer. If this bold statement is true – and I believe it is – then there are far-reaching and exciting implications for our primary classrooms. The challenge for us as teachers is to decide how to create the right conditions for young writers to thrive. This book attempts to help us make those decisions, not by pretending to have a magic formula but by turning quality educational research, and what some of the best minds in the field of human expertise tell us, into practical teaching and learning strategies that work.

For many years, scientists believed that our abilities were pre-determined by genetics: that our potential was limited by the fixed circuitry of our brains. Since the 1990s, however, researchers have established that our brains are far more adaptable than anyone ever imagined and we have a tremendous amount of control over what our brains can do. Anders Ericsson's research inspired the popular '10,000-hour rule', which suggests that anyone can reach expert level at anything if they practise for long enough (approximately ten years in real terms). Mozart, for example, was not born with the gift of perfect pitch. The gift he was born with, says Ericsson, was the ability to develop perfect pitch and pretty much everyone is born with that gift. This is an amazing and inspiring fact for anyone involved in education. We all have great potential for excellence; all we need is practice. Well, not just any practice. After all, any golfer knows that you don't get better at playing the game just by doing it over a long period of time. Some of us get worse! Ericsson says we need 'deliberate practice' which is more purposeful, thoughtful and focused. It is 'all about putting a bunch of baby steps together to reach a longer-term goal'.

This philosophy can apply to any field of human endeavour and, most certainly, to primary classrooms where children are learning to write. Granted, we don't have ten years to work with children in our primary schools but we do have at least seven. Also, our pupils are not in school all year round but the substantial amount of time committed to writing in most schools on a daily basis does, you have to say, present tremendous opportunity.

A long-term aim for primary writers

Part of mastery learning is about being clear about our long-term aim for developing writers in primary school and those baby steps that will take them there.

Simon Camby (2015) warns of the danger of becoming too subject-based when we think of mastery. This can lead to teacher tick lists, which serve little purpose, and to acceleration through content, which generates the kind of shallow learning that the National Curriculum in England (2014) was designed to avoid. The curriculum was designed to promote the study of fewer things in greater depth and, as such, is a written invitation to mastery learning.

In his book, *Mastery Depth in the National Curriculum*, Camby seeks to stimulate discussion in schools by pointing to a number of alternative ways of conceptualising mastery. In my view, he rightly focuses attention on how learners use and apply skills rather than on subject content. This is one set of definitions that Camby offers:

- **Shallow learning**: surface, temporary, often lost
- **Deeper learning**: sticks and can be used
- **Mastery learning**: can be transferred.

It is interesting that the Cambridge dictionary of English (2018) defines 'mastery' as 'complete control over something'. This chimes with Noel Burch's Conscious Competence Model of learning which says that we have to work through a conscious competence stage of learning – consciously thinking about and practising a skill – before we can enjoy unconscious competence. At this stage, we can pass control over this skill to our unconscious mind while we focus on other things. It just seems easy and we can do it without thinking about it. We are fluent in this skill.

Writing is perfect for mastery learning because the practise of skills, particularly personal targets, can take place across the curriculum. I suggest that our long-term aim for developing writers in primary school is mastery learning that can be applied to a wide range of contexts with independence and fluency.

Journey over destination

A huge amount of work is needed on the part of teachers (and the pupils themselves) to put young writers firmly on a mastery learning journey. It is a journey, though, and not a destination. As teachers we need to focus less on outcomes (measured by narrow assessment criteria) and more on process. This book will do just that: focus less on destination and more on the journey itself. What does mastery learning look like? What teaching and learning experiences do we want our pupils to have on a daily basis? I will consider in detail the baby steps children need to take towards their long-term goal and what help they need from their teacher along the way.

A checklist approach

Primary school teaching is a complex business. To begin with, there is the subject knowledge required to deliver appropriate sequences of work across perhaps 12 subjects. Then you must get to know the children you are teaching – in detail. What, for example, are their starting points, their relative abilities, their specific needs, their barriers to learning? Then you must have the skills to put this huge amount of knowledge to effective use in order to help bring about the required progress. All this, of course, must be done in the face of other factors which can be largely beyond our control, such as constantly shifting expectations, pressure from parents, school leadership or outside agencies, the children's behaviour for learning and mixed messages regarding best practice. Outcomes in this context can be highly uncertain.

Of course, teaching is not the only profession which places huge demands on the people who do the work. In fact, comparing the primary teacher's lot to that of somebody applying their expertise in a completely different field can be quite sobering. In his book, *The Checklist Manifesto: How to Get Things Right* (2011), Atul Gawande shares the heart-wrenching story of a three-year-old girl who fell into an icy fishpond while out walking with her parents in the Austrian Alps. She had been under water for half an hour when she was found and lifeless for an hour and a half by the time a surgical team got to work on her. However, her organs began to recover and she went home two weeks after the accident. By the age of five, she had recovered completely.

We can only marvel at the knowledge and expertise, the commitment and professionalism that the medical team demonstrated to bring what seemed such a hopeless cause to such a happy conclusion. How could a group of people in an ordinary community hospital – far removed from a large, cutting-edge academic medical centre – pull off something so enormously complicated? To save this one child, scores of people had to carry out thousands of steps correctly and in the right sequence, with very little margin for error. The norm is that people involved in drowning incidents such as this don't make it, and the difference in this case was something surprisingly simple: a checklist.

The checklist was put into the hands of the rescue teams as well as hospital staff so that everything was in place in advance to revive patients from cardiac arrest after hypothermia and suffocation, and the channels of communication were clear. The rescue of the three-year-old girl was the team's first success with the checklist in place. At least two other such rescues have taken place since.

Gawande charts other examples in which use of a simple checklist produced incredible results. They include helping pilots fly jet aeroplanes safely and ensuring huge commercial buildings – including skyscrapers – are built with incredible success. His point is that, in today's world, we have accumulated a vast amount of know-how and put it in the hands of some of the most highly trained, highly skilled and hard-working people in society. However, avoidable failures are common across many fields, from medicine to business, law to education.

Surely by now we have the combined know-how to make success the norm in education. Yet learning outcomes vary hugely from one school to the next, from one authority to the next. Perhaps we simply need to learn to deliver the benefits of what we know more consistently and reliably? Of course, using checklists for everything we do as teachers is neither practical nor desirable, but the checklist offers us a way of building on experience and taking advantage of people's knowledge in specific contexts. It could be hugely beneficial in an area of primary school teaching which has long presented considerable challenges: writing.

F STEPS

So what is this combined know-how we have amassed as a profession from successes and failures in the teaching of writing? Firstly, I wanted to take account of quality research designed to improve our understanding of how different aspects of pedagogy impact on children's learning. Secondly, I asked more than 30 peers in primary education – including experienced class teachers, English co-ordinators, head teachers and teaching and learning consultants – for their opinions. I simply asked them, 'What are the most important things a teacher needs to do in order to help children make good progress in writing?'.

As you might imagine, there were many different opinions about what constitutes good teaching of writing but a lot of commonality too. In fact, the responses could be distilled down to the following checklist (which, conveniently, can be coined as F STEPS). This checklist of important strands of learning will be explored in detail in the following chapters.

Feedback	Using feedback to empower children to become active partners in their own development
Skills	Routinely consolidating prior learning and teaching new writing skills in a logical progression
Talk and thought	Exploring literature and big questions, and thinking together to inspire quality writing
Engagement	Hooking children in to learning contexts so that they want to write
Practice	Using the principles of deliberate practice to develop writing skills for different contexts across the curriculum
Sequence	Putting these strands together to design effective units of work, from learning from authors to quality writing outcomes.

Planning for mastery learning

We have established that, to help children to reach their long-term aim, we need to be clear about the skills that they need to acquire. The National Curriculum in England (2014) sets out a skills progression for writing from Year 1 to Year 6. However, there are gaps. Some skills are implied rather than stated. For example, if there is no mention of paragraphing or Standard English in your year group, does that mean you don't need to teach it? Other skills or concepts that are not included are extremely useful because they help to underpin children's understanding of skills that *are* included. For example, does it make sense for children to do some work with regular and irregular verbs when writing in the simple past and simple present forms in advance of tackling the progressive form of verbs in Year 2?

Chapter 2 introduces a set of documents called Steps in Learning. Not only do they set out a fuller picture of the skills journey in each year group, which is especially important for newly qualified or new-to-year-group teachers, they also suggest a logical order in which to teach these **skills**. It is crucially important that children's new learning builds on their prior learning. Teaching skills out of sequence can only lead to confusion and hamper progress. If the Steps in Learning documents provide a long-term planning guide for teachers, setting out the baby steps young writers need to take in Years 1 to 6, the remaining F STEPS constitute the mission-critical help that teachers can give them along the way.

Feedback, the focus of Chapter 1, is essential to progress. Teachers need to prioritise formative conversations with and between children so that they know what they are doing well and how they can improve. Focusing these conversations on specific next steps over time can help children to take more and more responsibility for their own progress.

To learn more deeply, children also need to think more deeply. **Talk and thought** (Chapter 3) refers to opportunities we can give to children to think collectively with their classmates. Such collaboration enables pupils to discover and refine their own ideas and find a clear and assured voice that will strengthen their writing. It is also one way to maximise children's engagement in their learning. If children enjoy learning to be a better writer then more progress is possible, so teachers need to think carefully about such things as choosing the right texts and writing outcomes, making learning relevant and establishing a relaxed learning environment. **Engagement** is the focus of Chapter 4.

Ultimately, to become the best writer they can be, children have to practise their writing skills. We teachers need to make sure the **practice** they do is the right kind of practice – deliberate practice – and help to ensure they are ready for, and respond to, the challenge. Techniques like shared writing and guided writing are vital cogs in the process, as we discover in Chapter 5.

The planning pyramid

This is a lot to think about when sitting down to plan an effective sequence of learning, which is precisely why teachers need a practical way of drawing all these strands together. The planning pyramid (below) is designed to make the planning of mastery learning in English more systematic, by focusing teachers' minds at first on just three elements of the F STEPS checklist – skills, talk and thought and writing outcomes. It will be explored in detail in Chapter 6.

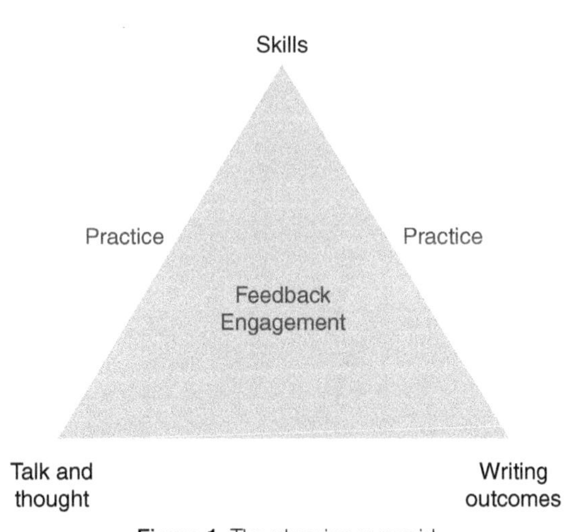

Figure 1 The planning pyramid

How to use this book

I have written this book in such a way that it can be read from start to finish, as a guide to mastery teaching in writing. Of course, each chapter can also be read independently and ideas put into practice individually. They can also be used as a training resource for teaching staff. I recommend that it should be read in its entirety so that the teaching and learning sequence featured in Chapter 6 can be fully understood. If you are free to do so, use the planning pyramid to make F STEPS your model for teaching and learning in English, or better still, adopt it as a whole-school approach so that teachers are in a position to support each other. You will be rewarded with more efficient use of planning and teaching time, and young writers who are hungry for progress.

1 Feedback

Feedback is one of the most effective tools teachers have at their disposal. To realise just how important it is, we only need to call to mind an occasion when we have enjoyed a degree of success in learning a new skill. If we are new to archery, for example, feedback from an experienced coach – evaluating our early attempts and telling us what we need to do to improve – is invaluable. The feedback aligns effort with outcome, refocusing the learner's performance – from side-on stance to release of the bow string – to achieve a goal: in this case, consistently shooting into the high-scoring zones in the centre of the target.

Meaningful positive feedback is a crucial factor in maintaining motivation and the consistent effort necessary to improve. Black and Wiliam (1998) concluded, 'the provision of challenging assignments and extensive feedback lead to greater student engagement and higher achievement'. Our challenge as teachers is to get the level of challenge right for our pupils and create a culture in our classrooms in which feedback is a top priority and used effectively to get children from where they are to where we want them to be. Are we using the right kind of feedback at the right times and, crucially, are we enlisting children in their own development as writers?

First of all, children have to want to improve. Creating and maintaining motivation is about planning and delivering an engaging curriculum: a curriculum the children find inspiring, interesting and relevant. It's about every child feeling like there is a lot expected of them and that progress they make towards set goals is worthwhile; this depends on the way teachers respond to their efforts. Carol Dweck's research (2000) distinguishes between students who receive feedback in the form of marks and results and those who are given comments relevant to the task. The latter see the feedback as helping them to improve and they tend to out-perform the former group, who see feedback as a way of comparing themselves with others. Fear of failure from feedback that ranks children can damage the self-esteem of low attainers and prevent higher attainers from taking risks.

If we get feedback right, children should feel increasingly positive and believe that they can improve. It needs to be task-specific and focused towards the attainment of a goal. The more specific the goal, the better, according to Locke and Latham (1984). In my work as a primary English consultant, I meet many teachers who worry about making similar comments in children's books week after week. This is understandable but our only concern should be whether or not feedback is having impact on learning. If we get the goal right in the first place then it will focus the pupils' attention so long as feedback is directed towards it. Small steps forward can then be celebrated and become very tangible for children, helping them develop a 'can-do' attitude to learning. Feedback unrelated to attainment of a goal – straying into general areas such as spelling, handwriting or volume of work (when for example, creating atmosphere is the intended learning) – is, unsurprisingly, not effective. Formative writing assessments that provide feedback directly to pupils should be part of our everyday teaching and learning (Graham, Herbert and Harris, 2015).

This chapter focuses on the power of feedback to motivate and guide children's progress against attainable goals. We explore how prioritising a continuous dialogue around these goals can help maximise progress by promoting positive thinking and reflection, and encouraging children to take increasing responsibility for their own learning.

Focus on a goal

Reaching our long-term aim – mastery learning that can be applied in a variety of contexts with independence and fluency – requires lots of hard work and commitment on the part of learners and teachers. Why should we bother? Well, beyond the teacher assessments, essays, assignments and exams that the education system puts in their path, learners need to develop their writing skills for the world of work. More than two thirds of salaried jobs require a substantial amount of writing. Getting a job in the first place demands effective communication through writing (application and CV), as does communicating professionally with colleagues, enhancing creativity and putting yourself in the frame for promotion.

Setting relevant goals

Of course, such long-term aspirations hold little relevance for the vast majority of primary-aged children. Breaking this down into logically sequenced 'baby steps' is a key role for schools and teachers.

Consider the following stages when setting goals:

- Each goal needs to have the appropriate level of challenge for each pupil, and each pupil needs to see its relevance and be motivated to take it. (The next chapter will consider how schools can organise these logically sequenced steps for whole-class teaching from year group to year group. Following a clear progression of skills across a school is liberating for teachers and tremendously powerful for children as they narrow the gap towards the long-term aim.)
- Making each step appropriate in terms of challenge involves knowing each child: their current knowledge and understanding and their next step. This knowledge can only come from careful tracking of children's prior development: a day-to-day use of observation, dialogue, marking and recording to chart children's progress in the skills journey of their year group.
- Teachers need to discuss and agree specific targets (or goals) with children, and then make sure that they understand what is expected of them in a specific task.
- Skills chosen as targets will often be the child's biggest barrier(s) to learning – the ones that, if achieved, will result in the biggest strides forward. These should be clearly evident from an audit of several pieces of writing.
- Consulting the children themselves about each target will ensure clarity and buy-in from the outset: the children know exactly what is expected of them and, hopefully, intend to do all they can to succeed.

Responding to pupils' efforts

When goals have appropriate challenge and teachers and pupils are committed to these goals, rapid progress is possible. Without commitment from teachers, the children can't even get off the starting blocks. Try to put yourself in the shoes of a child who is given a new writing target. The child tries his best to work at his target; after all, this is what he thinks will please his teacher. Imagine if, despite his best efforts, the teacher pays no attention to the target in her feedback, choosing instead to focus on other aspects of the child's writing in her marking. What is the impact on the child's motivation to achieve his goal? Let's imagine the very best-case scenario: the child re-doubles his effort towards the goal in week two. If, by the end of week two, the child has still received no acknowledgement of this effort – nothing to suggest whether or not he is making progress – then I would suggest that the target is rapidly becoming meaningless. It has already lost the power to motivate.

What must come first is quality teaching that enables children to take a good knowledge and understanding of concepts into application through writing. What must come next is the teacher devoting time and energy to specific feedback on children's goals so that they are in no doubt about their priorities as developing writers. Regular feedback on their targets – celebrating success and suggesting routes to improved application – can help pupils internalise what is expected of them and develop a desire for more progress. Remember, children have to want to make progress and such feedback on well-tailored goals is the key to enhancing commitment and increased effort. It is also the key to formative assessment and metacognition, which are routes to even bigger strides forward in learning.

Example goals

Despite being faced with the challenge of their age-related expectations, we have to acknowledge that some children's needs lie elsewhere – and be ready to address those needs. Some Key Stage 2 children, for example, may still be wrestling with the challenge of using full stops appropriately or making their sentences make sense: issues that present real barriers to their growth in confidence as writers.

In the next chapter, we will consider the need for children to be taught skills that help pave the way to age-related expectations. Key understanding can be consolidated and children who should have acquired certain skills by certain stages but haven't, can be identified. This process can also generate target areas for children. For example, a Year 3 child might need to work on staying on the same subject across several sentences before 'organising paragraphs around a theme'. He/she might need to work on punctuating one-clause sentences and using simple conjunctions before 'extending sentences with a wider range of conjunctions', or making appropriate tense choices before meeting the 'perfect form of verbs'.

Bringing the 'me' into cognition

If we are not careful, children can develop the idea that learning is the responsibility of other people. They might think: 'It's my teacher's job to teach, to get me to understand things and to mark my work so that I know if it is right or wrong, good or bad'. With this mindset, children can become passive recipients of education. They can in actuality make some progress but, if we are serious about the pursuit of deeper learning and mastery, we need to engage children in their own learning through formative assessment. Robert Fisher goes as far as to say that 'the main purpose of teaching is to empower students to become self-directed learners capable of taking responsibility for their own learning. Teachers can stimulate and support this by actively engaging children in their own learning through dialogue'.

Formative assessment

At its simplest, this is a two-way conversation between teacher and child in the form of formative assessment. Assessment is formative if it gives pupils the information they need to assess themselves and modify their learning behaviour. 'Feedback from teachers is helpful if it does not just say what was right or wrong, but helps pupils understand why. Improvement in learning is about change in learning behaviour. No change in behaviour – no improvement in outcomes' (Fisher).

Get this interaction right and the children's outcomes can also provide useful feedback to the teacher.

- Where has the teaching been successful?
- How does it need to be modified to meet the needs of pupils?

Teaching that is based on evidence in this way is more likely to meet with success than teaching based on tests or assumptions. 'Assessment becomes "formative assessment" when the evidence is actually used to adapt the teaching work to meet learning needs' (Black et al., 2002).

If cognitive learning is about the processing of subject knowledge, metacognition is the next level up. It is about knowledge of self and self-regulation. Flavell (1979) introduced the term 'metacognition' to refer to 'the individual's own awareness and consideration of his or her cognitive processes and strategies'. As Flavell says, bringing the process of learning to a conscious level can help children to be more aware of their own thought processes and enable them to gain control or mastery over the organisation of their learning. In other words, metacognition puts the 'me' into cognition. It is me going beyond the usual listening, doing, remembering and responding to others in the classroom; it is me thinking about my thinking and how I learn. Vygotsky (1962) argued that this is an essential factor in effective learning: gaining knowledge but also reflecting on that knowledge and gaining conscious control over it.

Feedback that fosters self-regulation is essential to the learning process. It is powerful because it enlists children as active partners in their own development. Their sense of ownership and control, in the right learning climate, leads to more focused thinking and children investing further effort in the task. Compare the teacher comment 'Some good use of apostrophes…' to 'These apostrophes make it clear that two words have been shortened. Are all of the apostrophes in your story needed?'. The latter comment encourages the pupil to do more thinking, to reflect on her own performance. It also makes her more aware of herself as a thinker and a learner: what she knows, what she has learnt, what she can and cannot do and how she can improve.

How often do we primary school teachers tell children that they must ask for help when they need it? Contrary to popular belief, self-regulated learners don't try to accomplish every task on their own, they frequently seek help from others when necessary (Butler, 1998). What sets self-regulated learners apart is that they not only seek advice from others but do so in order to make themselves more autonomous (Ryan et al., 2001). How do we promote this positive help-seeking behaviour in the classroom? We provide pupils with ongoing progress feedback that they can easily understand.

Implications for the classroom

After quality teaching of subject content, we should make feedback for self-regulation a big priority in our classrooms. Teaching children who are actively engaged in their own progress is like soaring through the waves in a sail boat with a fully active crew and a good wind, as opposed to trying your best to tack along with very little wind, doing everything yourself. You get a lot further with a lot more efficiency of effort! No-one is saying this is easy: giving and acting on feedback in this way requires skill on the part of pupils and teachers. For teachers, part of this skill is about staying on top of everyone's changing needs and providing timely feedback before frustration takes over and there is a detrimental impact on motivation. It is also about asking the right questions. If we want pupils to take responsibility for their own learning, we need to ask questions that get them thinking for themselves, to develop and use ideas and to develop self-awareness as learners.

Divert time from other tasks

The potential rewards are so great that we cannot afford to ignore them. We must find time in our incredibly busy timetables to prioritise activity that helps children to help themselves. It can make our teaching more efficient and more effective, but it's easier said than done when we consider all the other duties and responsibilities of primary teachers, isn't it? 'Devoting time and thoughts to feedback is aided when teachers automate many other tasks in the classroom and provide rich learning opportunities for all students and thus have the time and resources to be responsive to feedback' (Hattie & Jaeger, 1998). How could we do this?

Feedback, not marking

Perhaps we should stop referring to marking and start referring to different forms of feedback. Feedback routines need to be organised for maximum efficiency.

Teachers have three opportunities to give pupils feedback:

1 Before the writing process
2 During the writing process
3 After the writing process.

Feedback before the writing process

Feedback at this stage can be used to support children in organising their ideas and structuring their writing.

- Take this opportunity to talk to children who are struggling to see how their response to a writing task might roll out. Ask them to explain how they intend to implement any planning. Just articulating their thinking out loud will help to clarify the way forward.

- Some children will benefit from noting down what each paragraph will focus on. An opportunity to talk this through, with the purpose of the writing at the forefront of their minds, will help them to decide how the paragraphs will link together and create a flow of meaning.
- Focus children's minds on their personal writing goals. There is lots for children to think about when they embark on a writing task, not least the intended learning of that particular lesson or unit of work. If we're not careful, children can lose sight of the goals that will help them to take their next steps as a writer. Remember, these goals can represent either the biggest barriers to their development as writers or an appropriate challenge to take their writing forward. A conversation around how children intend to take action on their personal goals in this specific task can be a really powerful aid to progress.

Feedback during the writing process

Feedback during the writing process is by far the most powerful, especially when it is specific to personal goals. By intervening right at the moment when a child is making mistakes, we can reiterate teaching points, give advice on how targets can be achieved and support attempts to improve. The immediacy and personal nature of this feedback can make a huge difference to a child's confidence, especially those who struggle to engage in whole-class teaching sessions.

It makes sense then to give as many children as is practicable quality feedback while they are writing.

- Group children with a shared need for a guided writing session. Limit the group to a maximum of six so that lots of attention can be given to each child's efforts and consider pairing the children to promote dialogue during the session.
- Start by re-teaching the concept in question using an example related to the writing task (perhaps using a whiteboard). The children should be active participants in this, ideally reminding you of the teaching points and making suggestions, possibly following discussion with a partner. Children then begin to apply their learning while you take time to support each individual. Questioning is crucial here to prompt children's thinking as they try things and explore different possibilities in their writing. Welcome errors and use them to improve the understanding of all the children in the group.
- Give the focus children time to apply their learning independently before returning to check progress before the end of the lesson. You can use this time – just ten minutes or so – to provide similar oral feedback to other children in the class.

Feedback after the writing process

Prioritising feedback during the writing process lightens the marking load following the lesson and enables the teacher to use more feedback for immediate impact; to refocus children onto their goals and ask questions to deepen their thinking. Feedback after the writing process should not be overly burdensome for teachers. Every teacher knows the potential limitations of marking following the writing process. By the time they read the comments – if they do at all – children's minds are no longer engaged in the task and so hours of marking by teachers can lack relevance to the children. Also, timetable pressures can mean it's difficult to make time available for children to read and respond to written feedback. If we find ourselves writing detailed comments in children's books, we should stop and ask ourselves why we are doing it. What will the impact be?

Our feedback should be concise and goal-focused. It should help children to reflect on their own performance and stimulate further thinking on targets. It should ask questions that probe children's assumptions about their learning. There is no doubt that conversations with children have more impact on progress than comments in their books. However, paying attention to children's performance at this stage can also help to group children with similar needs. Guided writing sessions can then be very focused on specific goals and can facilitate children supporting each other in their attempts to improve, as well as receiving guidance from the teacher. It can also inform children's next efforts, so long as they are given time to reflect on the teacher's feedback.

- Consider adopting an OWL approach to feedback: Oral feedback, Written feedback and Light marking. As already outlined, try to give as much feedback as possible through focused conversations with children. Written feedback should be used selectively, indicating how a child has responded to a limited set of success criteria (which should always include their own personal targets). Success criteria let children know when they have achieved a learning goal. Light marking could involve the use of colour-coded highlighters to draw children's attention to what they have done well in relation to the criteria and what they could improve on.
- All three feedback formats have the common aim of engaging children in their learning by letting them know how they are doing, particularly against agreed goals or targets, and guiding their thinking towards further improvements. If marking work after a task is completed, try to do it as soon after the writing task as possible. Sharing such feedback immediately after a lesson at break time or lunch time gives you time to gather individuals or groups of children to reflect and respond, and enables you to clarify feedback through brief conversations.

Self- and peer-assessment

In time, such regular, goal-oriented feedback – during and after the writing process – will help children to become less reliant on their teacher telling them what they can and cannot do. Children begin to internalise their own goal posts and what they must do to score goals. It leads to understanding of content as well as the processes of learning, and to the child taking greater responsibility for his/her own learning. This purposeful dialogue between teacher and child is a form of 'thinking together' (explored in detail in a Chapter 3), which paves the way for self- and peer-assessment.

Enabling children to have meaningful dialogue with each other, and internally within their own minds, is the pinnacle of formative assessment. By routinely devoting time and energy to the sort of learning dialogue described above, we are creating the conditions in which children can begin to really thrive as independent, self-directed learners through self- and peer-assessment.

- **Self-assessment** is essential to learning if pupils are to understand for themselves whether they have reached a learning goal. It can also have an important ally in peer-assessment.
- **Peer-assessment** puts pupils into the role of 'teachers' and gives them opportunities to explain their thinking, as well as the strengths and weaknesses in a given piece of work, in a stress-free context.

Self-assessment

Building regular time for reflection into writing tasks can help to develop habits for effective learning, so long as children use it effectively. They need to be clear about what to focus on. As well as regularly proofreading as they write, pupils need to re-focus on their personal targets together with any specific success criteria set by the teacher during these brief opportunities. Reading their work out loud is an important technique here. It is well worth considering some other simple ideas for such reflection.

- Play two minutes of music to signal two minutes of self-reflection time. The children should be ready to tell their partner one idea they have had from their two minutes of self-reflection.
- Get the children to imagine that they are the teacher. What feedback would they give themselves?
- Ask the children to assess their performance against agreed success criteria. Be careful that this doesn't turn into a tick-box exercise. If children feel they have made progress against a specific criteria, perhaps they could record the paragraph(s) in which this progress can be found.

Encouraging and guiding children to reflect on their own understanding, successes or failures, is teaching them the skills of a successful learner. According to Howard Gardner (1983), people who have developed strong intrapersonal intelligence have a good sense of self and their abilities as a learner. If children depend solely on their teacher's approval, they will learn to rely on this feedback more than their own self-reflection. To prepare for secondary education and the adult world, they must learn to rely on themselves: on their own assessment of their progress. We need to get them into the right habits: routines of honest, reflective thinking that will set them up for life-long learning.

Peer-assessment

Regular practice at peer dialogue will enhance the self-talk that children need to become effective proofreaders. Allowing this sort of formative dialogue to widen and focus on specific targets, and ultimately the impact or otherwise of what has been written, also helps children to be more precise about their self-assessment.

- Give children an opportunity to read their work out loud to each other or to a group, or get them to swap books and have a peer read their work back to them. Either way, children become the reader of their own work. When text is read aloud in this way, it can make any mistakes quite obvious. Often children can 'hear' their mistakes far more easily than they can see them.
- Focus children's dialogue with one another on very specific criteria: personal targets or the objective of the day. If a child has the opportunity to explain their thinking to a peer, he/she will often think of his/her own ideas for further improvement.
- Consider developing children's coaching skills to use in regular formative dialogue with their peers. See Chapter 4 for more information on coaching for children.

Rising above the writing task

Self-reflection and peer-assessment have too often been afterthoughts – things you do at the end of a writing process. The trouble with this is that, if the children are moving on to a separate task or unit of work, it may be difficult or impossible for them to act upon any ideas that come out of this reflection. It is no good for children to reach some useful conclusions about what they need to do to improve their use of direct speech, if their next writing project is a set of instructions! To be effective, time needs to be devoted to this sort of reflection and it needs to be timely: it needs to pave the way to further learning, taking account of the merits and shortcomings of a child's efforts so far. It is also much more effective if it is focused on something tangible – on the next steps towards a long-term aim.

The helicopter task

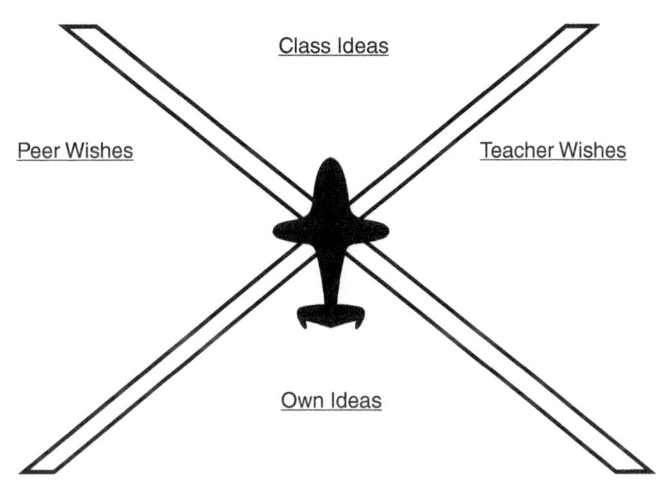

Figure 2 A suggested helicoptering pro-forma for use in classrooms

Figure 2 shows a technique that facilitates this sort of formative dialogue. The idea is that, following a piece of writing (possibly during the next English lesson), children begin to look forward to editing, redrafting or moving on to the next part of a writing task which the teacher has already outlined. Before doing so, they get the opportunity to 'helicopter' or rise above the task and take in their learning 'landscape'. They reflect on their own writing and make some decisions about how they intend to go forward by thinking about the teacher's feedback and what they have learnt from a conversation with a peer. This peer-to-peer conversation involves reading their work aloud to each other and discussing how they have responded to the task and any progress, or lack of it, towards personal targets. A printable version of Figure 2 can be found in Appendix 1.

Several children are also chosen to share their work with the whole class, stimulating a discussion on what they have done well and what they could do to improve. In the light of the purpose of the piece of writing, any use of skills currently being studied can be aired, questions arising from the text explored, alternative expressions tried and comparisons made for accuracy and impact. All this rich analysis and dialogue helps children – particularly those who can sometimes struggle for their own creative ideas – reflect on their own writing and think about how they can improve. It may also prompt children to think of their own new ideas. The children get the opportunity to capture their new thinking under the four headings of the 'helicoptering' grid. The more explicit pupils can be in recording their intentions – ideally in the form of expressions, phrases or sentences they intend to use – the more useful the activity in terms of informing their subsequent writing.

Ideas in practice

Name: Helen Cain
Teaching level: Year 2
School: St Thomas of Canterbury

At the start of a unit of work on story writing, the children began with a traditional and familiar tale, *Cinderella*. They re-told the story verbally and we used drama and role play to remind them of the main elements of the story. After looking at a range of pictures to sequence the story, the children identified how many paragraphs they would need to write in order to retell it. This was intended to simplify the task as they were also having to juggle a lot of new concepts. I was asking them to try to showcase their new learning about possessive apostrophes. They are also trying to assimilate lots of new spelling rules and key words and they are being asked to organise their work into paragraphs. They are accumulating a lot of skills for their toolkit! The familiar context of a traditional tale helped to facilitate their learning.

After they had planned out their paragraphs using a story planner, the children embarked upon their writing project, eager to write their ideas down. The following day, they used the helicoptering technique to reflect on their writing skills. Were they effective in retelling the story in paragraphs? Did they remember their spelling rules and key words? Were they able to find an opportunity to show their command of using the possessive apostrophe (whilst retaining previous knowledge about contractions and plurals!)?

Isla reflected on one of her paragraphs and then her partner read it and completed the 'peer reflection' section. Her partner's wishes indicated that, at times, Isla hadn't written on the lines. At this age, I was also giving them individual and whole-class guidance about exactly what to look for: the 'teacher wishes' section indicates the whole-class objectives and sums up what we have been working on over the last week/weeks. In this case, I was re-emphasising the importance of chunking sections of the story up into paragraphs and using the possessive apostrophe correctly.

In the 'class wishes' section, the children join in with a whole-class discussion to tell me some general issues they have found with each other's writing. The children then looked at their work again with fresh eyes, having looked at it from a number of perspectives. They write down their 'own ideas'. Isla wanted to improve her spelling and she noticed that she had missed out a question mark. She then re-drafted the paragraph with these amendments and the other three sections of the helicopter in mind. She felt in control of all aspects of the toolkit and she knew how to evaluate and improve her writing. The final piece reflects a mindful re-drafting of a paragraph that was much improved. The writing was on the lines, the spelling was improved, she included a missing question mark and she used a possessive apostrophe appropriately. What *Cinderella* story would be complete without reference to Cinderella's glass slipper?

Things to think about

- Do you expect children's writing toolkit to grow as they accumulate grammar, handwriting and spelling skills?
- Can you see an opportunity to use helicoptering to help children evaluate and improve their writing?

Figure 3 shows one child's first draft and Figure 4 shows the same child's re-draft, following the helicoptering reflection. It is clear how the helicoptering activity helped the child to arrive at specific intentions for her writing. She then took ownership of these points for improvement – including making appropriate use of a possessive apostrophe and question mark – and used these effectively in her re-draft.

Helping children to assess their own work in relation to specific learning targets is something they will need to practice regularly. After agreeing appropriate targets with children, teachers need to make sure that each pupil understands what is expected of them in a specific task. They need to be able to visualise what progress against a target looks like. This involves modelling and, ideally, sharing examples of the sort of 'destination' writing that a sequence of learning is leading towards. This can be as simple as the product of a shared writing session or an effective piece of writing from a previous cohort of children. Better still, it can be very helpful if children are given time to analyse several pieces of work of varying quality. They can then work together to rank the work, justifying their thinking.

A classroom rich in opportunities for formative dialogue engages children in thinking and pushes for depth in thinking. It makes children's thinking and learning transparent as it happens and gives teachers opportunities to deal with misconceptions before they get in the way of future learning. Robert Fisher says, 'This process is not simply about helping children improve their critical and creative thinking. It is also about fostering among them a belief that, with more active involvement in their own learning, they can make real and sustained progress'.

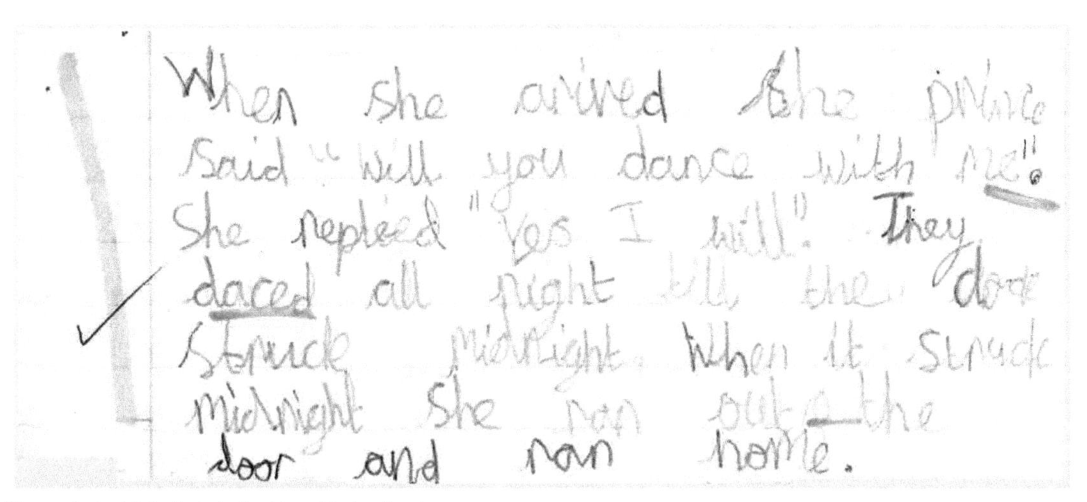

Figure 3 A child's first draft of her *Cinderella* story

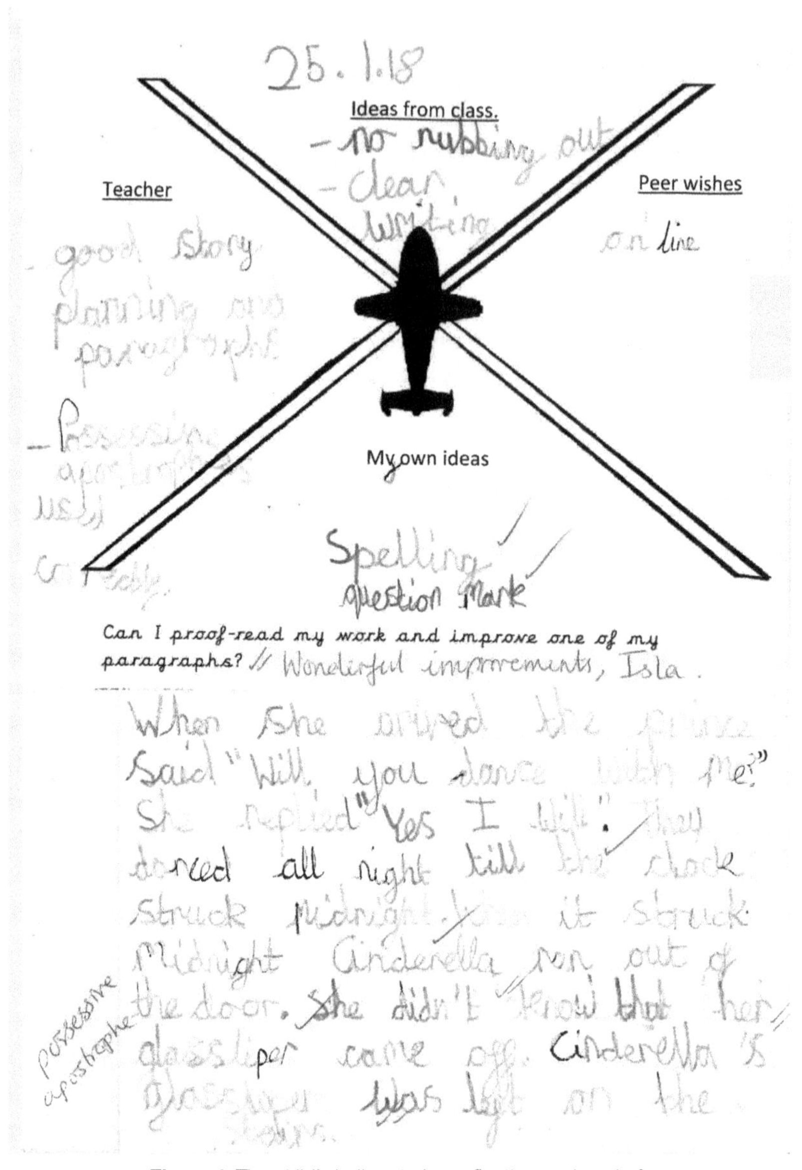

Figure 4 The child's helicoptering reflection and re-draft

Developing growth mindsets

For young children, the language we choose when giving feedback is vital to both their cognitive and emotional development. It is very important here to note the biological differences between infants and juniors, and indeed adults.

The adult brain has five frequencies of brainwaves, the lowest frequency being delta waves and the highest frequency being gamma waves. In the brains of young children, the two lowest frequency brainwaves – delta and theta – predominate. In adult brains, delta waves are associated with deep sleep while theta waves are associated with imagination or being under hypnosis. During this state, information can be directly downloaded into the subconscious mind. This means that in the first six to seven years of life, a child's brain predominantly operates below consciousness and is highly programmable.

During those years, Bruce Lipton explains in his book *The Honeymoon Effect* (2013), a child is unable to intellectually understand that verbal barbs are not true. A parent's negative comments, such as 'you are bad' or 'you can't do this', regardless of intention, are downloaded as truth just like files on a computer's hard drive. Only after the age of seven can a child rationalise a comment like 'you don't deserve that toy'. Instead of being downloaded into his subconscious, a child can consciously evaluate the comment, thinking of a range of reasons why Dad might have said it – 'my dad's angry because I was mean to my brother'.

'Nature has endowed babies' and young children's brains with the ability to download an unimaginable number of behaviours and beliefs very quickly' (Lipton, 2013). This is both a huge opportunity and a responsibility. It means that children up to the age of seven are particularly in need of positive feedback. Of course, this does not mean that dialogue relating to areas for improvement is sacrificed for limitless praise.

Imagine yourself giving feedback to a child who has responded to a writing task quite poorly. Perhaps he/she slipped into third-person narrative when he/she was supposed to be writing in role as a character. What should you say? Your responses could be anywhere between 'A great piece of writing. You really got me excited with your ideas' to 'This is awful. You're going to get nowhere if you write like this'. The first response creates a false reality and the child learns nothing while the second response is likely to damage the child's self-esteem and motivation to work hard at improving. There is, of course, a middle way. 'I love the effort you put into making your story exciting. When did YOU stop being involved in the story? What can we do about this?'. Couched in positive terms, this feedback presents a way forward – one that is only attainable through focused practice.

We want children to understand that a good process leads to good learning. Feedback in the classroom needs to recognise the positives (particularly if a child has put lots of effort into their work) while making it clear how they can improve. It should use errors as opportunities for further learning. In this way, we are focusing children not on specific outcomes but on the process of getting better. We are developing growth mindsets. By focusing children's thinking and effort on the next 'baby step' they need to take to make them a better writer, and celebrating when they are taken, we develop a culture of improvement. Children believe that they can improve and, with effort and constructive feedback from their teacher, they will.

A whole-school approach

Research completed by Professor John Hattie, Director of the Melbourne Educational Research Institute at the University of Melbourne (2003), suggests that expert teachers believe that every child can achieve the learning objective. Of other characteristics he found were common among expert teachers, the following relate directly or indirectly to assessment and feedback:

- Create an optimal classroom environment for learning which is rich in feedback and welcomes errors. Children feel at ease about making mistakes in front of their peers

- Monitor learning and provide lots of relevant and useful feedback on children's efforts
- Look for evidence of children who have not learned, or not making progress, and adapt their teaching accordingly
- See children's progress as feedback about the effect they are having on learning.

We cannot realistically expect everyone to be an 'expert' teacher, so what we need in a school are opportunities to learn from others' best practice and whole-school systems, which make this important work easier for some and more consistently applied across the year groups. We have explored the second bullet point above in some detail, concluding that feedback needs to relate to progress against specific learning goals or targets of each individual child and, with the aim of encouraging self-directed learning, involving regular opportunities for self- and peer-assessment. The practice of setting targets with children – based on careful audits of their work, supporting work towards them through ongoing dialogue and guided writing, assessing and tracking progress – needs to be uniform across the school.

Such consistency lays the foundation for enhancing progress and attainment. Teachers, particularly those with less experience, can be confident that they are 'doing things right' and, given the opportunities, can discuss issues, support each other and celebrate successes from a shared perspective. Children benefit from the clarity of their working relationships and not having to re-learn a different regime each year. Also, English co-ordinators and senior leaders can much more easily monitor and manage progress in teaching and learning. A united teaching team that believes in what it is doing and is pulling in the same direction, particularly with regard to this all-important area of assessment and feedback, is in a much stronger position to take a school's English provision forward.

It is worth finishing with a final reflection from John Hattie (2012) on his research: 'The remarkable feature of the evidence is that the greatest effects on student learning occur when teachers become learners of their own teaching, and when students become their own teachers'.

Reflection points

- Have you set achievable targets or goals for your pupils?
- Do you provide extensive and meaningful feedback relating to children's targets to help them to make progress in writing?
- Do you facilitate a constant goal-oriented dialogue with a view to helping children become self-directed learners who take responsibility for their own progress?
- Do your school leaders empower you to save time with other routines, such as marking after writing, in order to prioritise this dialogue?
- Does the feedback you provide prompt further thinking and help children to understand not only what they have done well or badly but how they can improve?
- Do you give children regular opportunities to reflect on their learning through self- and peer-assessment to help them become self-reliant and establish habits for successful proofreading and life-long learning?

- Can you see an opportunity to use the helicopter task as a simple child-friendly format for formative dialogue aimed at helping children to reflect on their writing so far and make decisions about improving their ongoing writing?
- Are you maximising progress by using feedback to develop growth mindsets and a culture of improvement in your classroom?
- Does your school drive improvement in English through whole-school approaches to assessment, target setting and feedback?

2
Skills

Our long-term aim as teachers of writing is mastery learning that can be transferred to a variety of contexts with independence and fluency. This requires learners and teachers devoting lots of time and energy to the acquisition of a wide range of skills, and the practice of those skills. We look to the government of the day for guidance on the writing skills appropriate for children in each year but, ultimately, it is the responsibility of schools to design their own curriculum and organise the skills that need to be practised in order to lead our learners to where we want them to be. Careful thought is needed for decisions on *what* needs to be taught, from spelling and handwriting to grammar and composition, as well as *how* it needs to be taught.

Today's schools have more freedom to decide on *how* they want the English curriculum to be taught than they have had for many years. Subsequent chapters will consider the *how* in detail: how schools and teachers can make best use of pupil talk, promote deeper thinking on the part of pupils, ensure effective skills practice and plan creative learning sequences in pursuit of mastery learning. This chapter will focus on the *what*.

A culture of consolidation

The pedagogy of English teaching has a lot to learn from that of mathematics, not least because of the importance that is attached to basic skills. For many years, careful thought has been given to identifying the skills that underpin much of the primary mathematics curriculum. It is widely recognised that children will struggle to make the desired progress in other areas of the subject without being relatively sound in their understanding of number bonds, place value, mental calculation methods, and so on. As a result, daily oral and mental activities have been devoted to these areas to consolidate learning. This has been the norm in primary schools rather than the exception.

Compare this to children's experiences in English in recent years. Have they been given the same routine opportunities to learn and relearn fundamentally important skills? For many schools the answer is 'no', yet the principle is the same. Knowledge and understanding of the full stop, for example, and word classes like nouns and verbs are hugely important building blocks for accurate and confident writing, and they underpin the learning of more advanced concepts as children move through the year groups.

Developing a culture of consolidation – in which prior learning is routinely reviewed – is crucial if we are to take the majority of children with us as we address the demands of our primary curriculum. This begins with systematic phonics teaching. The constant consolidation of previous learning that is required as children move between the stages points the way for our teaching for deeper learning and mastery in writing across the school. Mastery learning involves breaking down content into a clear series of sequential steps. Each is pursued until learners can show they are ready to move on. Extra tuition and support is put in place for those children not reaching an expected standard. Of course, this process is a lot harder than it sounds and, for it to be successful, the learning needs to be meaningful, lively and engaging.

Learning to read *write*

Firstly, it is useful to consider the link between writing and reading, particularly right at the beginning of the primary school journey when children are taking their first steps as readers and writers. We cannot make decisions about the early development of writing skills in isolation from the development of reading and phonics.

Phonics

Using phonics as the overriding strategy for teaching reading is not universally popular. Some educationalists believe that other elements of the so-called 'searchlights model' should not be ignored. Certainly, the ability to pick up on contextual clues is increasingly important in Key Stage 2. However, the inverse relationship between reading and spelling is clear. When we read, we translate a printed word into sound by breaking down (or decoding) the symbols used to represent sounds and using the pattern of those letters to work out how to say it. To spell, we do the reverse: taking sounds and converting them into printed words using our phonological awareness and understanding of word patterns. These require a developing understanding of letter-sound correspondence and then of within-word patterns, syllable structure and derivations.

The weight of recent research makes a compelling case for systematic phonics teaching. For example, a ten-year study took place in West Dunbartonshire, the second most deprived area in Scotland, which became the first authority to state it had eradicated illiteracy among school leavers. It highlighted the superior benefits of a strong and structured programme of synthetic phonics over traditional phonics teaching strategies. There is little doubt that, when phonics is taught in a structured way, from the easiest sounds through to the most complex, it is the most effective way of teaching young children to read. Hence the UK Government's decision to introduce the phonics screening check at the end of Year 1 from 2012.

Due to the close relationship between phonics and spelling, writing as well as reading skills stand to benefit considerably from the power of systematic phonics teaching. Researchers estimate that around 84 per cent of words in the English language are predictable using phonics (Hanna et al., 1966). Therefore, as long as writing is taught alongside reading through phonics, it follows that the more robust the phonics teaching, the better prepared children are for accurate spelling. Explicit phonics instruction helps children to learn patterns and gives them a framework for spelling that increases their chances of being able to apply these spelling patterns accurately.

Most common words

Clearly, other strategies are needed for the more irregular words in the English language. Only 100 words account for approximately 50 per cent of words in English print (Fry et al., 1985). The first 25 of these make up about a third of all words used in reading and writing. It makes sense that early reading and spelling instruction should focus on these frequently used words, many of which have irregular spelling patterns. This involves helping children to become familiar with groups of 'exception' words and creating an expectation in their minds that not all words will fit the usual patterns.

In other languages like German and Italian, you can rely upon the idea that one letter represents one sound. In English, this is far from the case: there are more than 400 sounds representing the 44 phonemes. Words like *was*, *said* and *do*, for example, all of which are on the most common 100 words list, contain unusual grapheme-phoneme correspondence: some of the letters don't sound the way we expect them to. In the word *said*, for example, the *ai* grapheme sounds like the *e* in *bed*... and all this when just when the children thought they had to key to unlock the code!

This is tricky for children, at least initially, so what can teachers do to help? Firstly, we can group words to be learnt by spelling pattern, where possible: for example, *here*, *there* and *where*; *two*, *twenty* and *twelve*. Most irregular words contain some phonetically regular parts so we can help children to recognise parts of words which are regular and parts which are not. Children can be taught to pronounce irregular words as they are spelled (such as Wed-nes-day) and given opportunities to practise spellings to help them to memorise patterns. Practice can include tracing words, saying the name of each letter as it is traced, and closing their eyes when spelling the word before checking. Using mnemonics can also be very useful to help children memorise irregular spellings: PEOPLE eat oranges, pigs like eggs; WhERE did you go? HERE, there and everywhere; and you hEAR with your EAR.

Attaching meaning to new words being learnt will help children with their writing. It enables children to store words and retrieve them from their working memories when they use the word again. Adding actions to words can also help children associate meaning with spellings. For example, you could make a triangular roof shape above your head to demonstrate the word *house*.

Take a look at Figure 5 below, the Year 1 common exception words, and think about how you might group them and which might lend themselves to physical prompts to aid memory.

Year 1 common exception words													
the	to	were	his	me	be	we	so	here	love	one	friend	push	house
a	are	was	has	you	he	no	by	there	come	once	school	pull	our
do	today	is	I	your	she	go	my	where	some	ask	put	full	of

Figure 5 Year 1 common exception words

Read, write link

The synergy between reading and writing does not end with phonics. All teachers recognise that the children who really thrive as writers are usually those who read widely. The impact of children habitually reading for pleasure both inside and outside school cannot be overstated. Ofsted's *Moving English Forward*, a training resource for teachers of English in primary schools published in 2012, contained a particularly sobering slide. It read, 'Being more enthusiastic about reading, and a frequent reader, was more of an advantage on its own than having well-educated parents in good jobs... finding ways to engage students in reading may be one of the most effective ways to leverage social change' (PISA, 2002).

According to Save the Children (2014), the degree of inequality in reading levels for children aged around ten is higher in England than in almost all other developed countries. By the final year of compulsory schooling, the reading skills of English children from disadvantaged backgrounds are on average two and a half years behind those from the most affluent homes (Jerrim, 2012). Thankfully, research evidence suggests that reading for pleasure has enjoyed something of a resurgence in recent years. Nearly six in ten UK children surveyed by the National Literacy Trust in 2016 said that they enjoyed reading either very much or quite a lot. This is heartening but the stakes are so high that schools cannot afford to take their eye off this particular ball and we must reflect each year on whether we are doing everything we can to promote wider reading. The Trust's research also highlights the link between enjoyment of reading and attainment – in terms of spelling and grammar as well as reading. Ten-year-olds who enjoy reading have a reading age 1.3 years higher than their peers who don't enjoy reading, rising to 2.1 years for 12-year-olds.

This list is by no means exhaustive but here are some ideas for promoting reading for pleasure in school:

- Whole-class or whole-school themed months or half terms. For example, specific authors or books could be celebrated during October, the 'month of magic'.
- Paired reading sessions in which children get to read and discuss a book with a friend. This is great for bringing a social element into what is usually a solitary activity.
- Model reading yourself. Be seen to be a passionate reader. Read children's books and be ready to talk to children, sharing your enjoyment and enthusiasm as well as your challenges with reading a particular book.
- Regularly make books or magazines to showcase children's writing and make them available for other children to read.
- Borrow a book for a friend. Ask children to use the school library to borrow a book they think one of their friends will like. They have to think actively about why they are choosing a book.
- Establish a recommendations wall on which children, and staff, can post their recommended reads and their responses to other people's recommendations. This can also be done successfully through digital sites like Pinterest.
- Organise a regular book exchange. Children get the opportunity to bring in books that they have read, and no longer want, to swap after discussion and recommendations.
- Regularly read the introduction, first chapter or blurb of a book to get children interested in reading it.

For lots more great ideas to inspire young readers, take a look online at the Scottish Book Trust's Big Book Bash.

Teaching and learning for reading development will affect writing development and vice versa, so decisions about curriculum need to be made with this in mind. In some US states, the two are still taught as very distinct disciplines. However, research evidence in recent years suggests the relationship is a powerful one. Fundamentally, both are meaning-making activities: a reader is faced with a text and makes meaning from it and a writer is faced with a blank page and makes meaning through text.

A child's literacy development is dependent on this interconnection between reading and writing. In practice, this means that reading (and speaking and listening) can be used as a springboard for writing projects, and writing can be used as a way to understand reading. One way of exploiting this synergy

Reading benefits from writing	Writing benefits from reading
Phonemic awareness (the understanding that words are developed from sound 'chunks') develops as children read and write new words.	Phonics skills or the ability to link sounds together to construct words are reinforced when children read and write the same words.
Practice in the process of writing their own texts helps children analyse the pieces that they read.	Writing involves transmitting knowledge in print and reading is a major source of knowledge.
The way children use language and conventions in writing can help them better understand an author's construction of his or her texts.	Ideas from reading inform creative writing.
Spelling and handwriting instruction improves reading word recognition (Berninger et al., 2002).	There is a high positive correlation between reading comprehension ability and the quality of writing composition (Berninger et al., 2002).

Figure 6 Reading benefits from writing and writing benefits from reading

is to ask children for written responses to comprehension questions about a shared text. In this way, critical reading is being practised through writing about reading. Tasking children to summarise the ideas from a text in their own writing, write a retelling of a familiar text, as well as using texts as a model and a source of ideas for their writing, are ways in which writing projects can be strengthened through careful, critical reading. The use of quality texts to inspire quality writing will be explored in detail in later chapters.

Another way in which teachers can use reading skills to enhance writing is to develop children's proofreading and self-assessment techniques. Fundamentally, what we write is written to be read, but do we always give our pupils an audience other than the teacher? In Chapter 1, we looked at the importance of peer-assessment and of children hearing their work read out loud. It casts them in the role of reader (or audience) for their own writing and enables them to hear mistakes. Such dialogue can improve their self-talk so that children can be more precise and diagnostic in their self-assessment, recognising what they need to change in order to improve.

Speaking and listening are integral to reading and writing. We commonly use the phrase 'writer's voice' without a second thought. We need to make sure we give it a second thought, not only to fulfill a requirement of the national expectation relating to reading out or performing their own writing but also to help children to be reflective writers and to discover their own ideas and opinions through talk. Extended talk, if used correctly, promotes deeper thinking and can aid the writing process. In Chapter 3, we will look at how we can use talk for best effect.

The literacy legacy

Because schools rely so much on government guidance for *what* needs to be taught, it is worth reflecting upon the challenge presented to children and teachers by the current National Curriculum in England. It is also useful to recognise the legacy that previous regimes have left in our schools.

Many would argue that the preoccupation with text-level skills development in the Government's Primary Framework for Literacy (2006) resulted in a lack of rigour at word and sentence level. It was not uncommon to find Year 6 children who were quite proficient at putting together a newspaper article which matched all text-level expectations but exposed significant issues with spelling or sentence construction. The grammar skills children were taught tended to be studied in a random manner as they occurred in different genres. Pupils got to know about imperative or 'bossy' verbs during a unit of work on instructions; past tense during a unit on recounts but little thought was given to building new skills onto what children already knew in a logical progression. You could also argue that a preoccupation with having children recognise genre features – and often lots of them – and use them in their writing prioritised technique at the expense of a genuine concern for using language for meaning and impact.

Teaching grammar

The National Curriculum England, introduced into primary schools in 2014, raised the bar considerably for spelling and sentence construction skills. Never before had English schools been clearer on what was expected of children in terms of spelling, grammar and punctuation in each year group, from 1 to 6. Perhaps, as teachers respond to the pressures of SPAG tests and external moderation, there is once again a risk of prioritising technique at the expense of audience and purpose – and enjoyment.

What is the point of teaching grammar in primary school, anyway? A number of studies (Hillocks, 1984; Wyse, 2004; Andrews et al., 2006) suggest there is little or no point as they found no evidence of grammar teaching having a positive impact on children's writing. I think we need to think very carefully about what we are setting out to do when we teach grammar concepts to children. Are we simply seeking to meet the requirements of the National Curriculum, almost treating the age-related expectations as ends in themselves? Or are we genuinely using these objectives to help children become better communicators through writing?

In 2015, a group of acclaimed children's authors, including Carnegie medalists Tim Bowler and Tanya Landman, wrote to the then education secretary, Nicky Morgan, to complain about the damaging effects of primary teachers steering children towards 'too elaborate, flowery and over-complex language' to meet assessment criteria. They argued that the National Curriculum assessment criteria had become a prescription for how children should write and was having 'quite adverse effects on their writing skills'. Cecilia Busby, the fantasy adventure author who spearheaded the protest, said children were constantly being asked by teachers and teaching assistants to add subordinate clauses or use more interesting words like *wonderful* and *enormous* instead of simple words like *good* and *big*. They are told to avoid words like *and* and *said* in favour of getting words like *additionally* and *exclaime*d into their work whenever possible.

Busby said that more complicated words are being presented as 'better' alternatives so that children 'fail to understand the nuances of their use, and also fail to realise that they are relatively unusual', and that 'they are used sparingly in good writing'. Children's author John Dougherty, who was chair of the Society of Authors' children's writers and illustrators group at the time, added his concern that 'We're teaching them [children] that it means stuffing writing with adjectives, rather than that good writing is about communication, and will vary depending on what you're trying to communicate, what kinds of emotion you're trying to stir up, what kind of character you're trying to put into their minds'.

Their argument is not against National Curriculum descriptors themselves as they accept that children's vocabulary and sentence structure becomes more complex as their writing develops. Their problem is when this is turned into a form of mark scheme which rewards children more for using more complicated words rather than simple ones or using a subordinate clause instead of not using one. They have a point, don't they? I'm sure we can all identify with the danger of not heeding the warning from these authors: 'We risk producing a generation of children who believe that a sentence such as "I bounded excitedly from my cramped wooden seat and flung my arm gracefully up like a bird soaring into the sky" is always better than "I stood and put my hand up"'.

So where does this leave us? The age-related expectations in each year group are the criteria upon which children's writing progress in English schools is measured so, like them on not, they have to be central to our practice. We just need to remember that, as the authors argue, use of vocabulary and parts of speech should always be subservient to a clear, fluent style that enables a writer to achieve a particular purpose. Developing understanding of the underpinning skills can really enhance writing outcomes so long as this work sits within a learning sequence which emphasises their use and application in meaningful writing tasks with clear purpose. If children's experience of grammar is through discreet circling, underlining and inserting activities, this will not give them the skills they need to communicate in a range of situations, nor motivate them as writers.

We all share a joy of language and using it for a multitude of reasons – socialising with friends, sharing jokes and stories, singing songs, and so on. Grammar teaching can be part of this joy of language. It doesn't have to be characterised by dull, repetitive drill. Again and again in my own practice, I witness children's fascination with unlocking the 'secrets' of the language we all use every day without thinking about it, and enjoying experimenting with those parts of speech in their own writing.

Thankfully, we have the work of Debra Myhill and her associates at Exeter University. They dispute the findings of the above-mentioned research on the basis that it largely focused on the effects of discrete grammar courses on writing. Myhill's research found strong evidence that the right kind of grammar teaching does improve children's writing skills: it makes a compelling case for teaching grammar within a purposeful writing context, creating opportunities for developing writers to explore how written text works. Writing is seen as a form of design and language as putty. Aspiring writers can shape it, and manipulate it in an infinite number of ways. They can have fun with language!

Frankly, this research provides the inspiration we all need to teach today's English curriculum in ways that are meaningful and enjoyable for children and teachers alike. If we get it right, it is likely that children will also perform well in SPAG tests. This is because they have had to engage more fully with the skills, thinking more deeply about them. However, the converse is not true. Prioritising skills development for SPAG tests, the means rather than the end, will not result in improved writing.

Clearly, a lot depends on *how* grammar is taught. Fundamentally, we are on the road to mastery learning in our primary classrooms if the following are in place:

- children want to write
- children have something to say and a reason for saying it
- children have the skills that will help them to say it.

We will consider this in more detail, with reference to Myhill et al.'s exciting research, in Chapter 5. First, we need absolute clarity on *what* grammar skills should be taught.

Deeper learning through logical progression

Along with reading and spelling, sentence construction is another crucial foundation stone for confident writing. Like the teaching of phonics, there needs to be a step-by-step progression for children: a logical progression that allows children to assimilate new concepts with their existing understanding of English. If this understanding includes a robust idea of what a sentence is, and can be, then it will be much easier for children to process information about unfamiliar grammatical concepts and link it to what they already know. If you like, the new learning can be anchored by their understanding of sentence construction. Without that strong sense of a sentence, the considerable content of today's writing curriculum can become a confusing whirl of concepts in children's minds.

These are good reasons why vocabulary, grammar and punctuation skills should be uppermost in a teacher's mind as they sit down to plan units of learning. Add to this the fact that it is always possible for teachers to provide the right contextual writing opportunities for applying newly-learnt grammar skills, and their importance in terms of assessment. Even then, we haven't fully made the case for teachers to make skills the driver for units of planning. Consider the likely consequences if we don't.

What if we allowed genre or writing form to drive those planning decisions, as was the case for most schools under the Primary Framework for Literacy (2006)? It is quite possible to 'cover' the English curriculum in this way but in what order? Alternatively, what if we allowed the texts used to deliver the curriculum to dictate matters? The same issue arises: the order in which grammar objectives are introduced to children would be somewhat random. Children would study concepts as they occur in the genre or text being studied, in the order that those genres or texts are organised in long-term planning. Well, so what? Does the order matter? Yes, it most certainly does. We all need our learning to be structured into logical steps if we are going to make progress towards a longer-term aim. To use a tennis example, it wouldn't make any sense to learn how to perform a slice backhand before learning how to hold the racket properly. Similarly, if you were teaching mathematics in Year 4, you wouldn't consider teaching counting in hundredths before place value or converting units of measure before mental multiplication and division.

Today's primary school teachers need a very good understanding of curriculum content to teach effectively. However, the concepts in each year group's expectations for writing are only part of the picture. Teachers also need to know the steps that will lead to understanding of these concepts. For example, what knowledge and understanding do Year 5 children need before they can 'use the perfect form of verbs to show time and cause'? They need a robust knowledge of verbs and an understanding of other verb tenses, including the simple and progressive forms.

Similarly, what knowledge and understanding do Year 4 children need before they can 'use fronted adverbials…'? They need to understand the function of adverbs and know that they can be used to signal such things as *how*, *when* and *where* an action occurs. Before that, they need to be robust in their knowledge of verbs – the action words themselves. Grammar learning is cumulative. Ignoring these steps and teaching directly to age-related expectations will save teachers lots of time and energy in the short term but will ultimately be counterproductive. It would be like building on sand. Likewise, teaching these concepts in the wrong order would do nothing to help children build the repertoire of skills and confidence they need to write successfully in different contexts.

It is particularly important for NQTs and new-to-year group teachers to be aware that there is a bigger picture to good writing that goes beyond age-related expectations (ARE). There are lots of underpinning skills that children need first and we ignore these at our peril. In the same way that children need a logical progression of skills in order to develop mastery in mathematics, they need a logical progression of grammar and sentence construction skills in order to have the toolkit they need to 'design' increasingly sophisticated texts.

The Steps in Learning for writing

Figure 7 shows the Steps in Learning for writing in Year 4 (find them for all year groups 1–6 in Appendix 2). The 'steps' are intended for teacher use only and amount to a long-term plan for writing. The numbering of the concepts in the Vocabulary, Grammar and Punctuation section suggests an order in which they should be taught. Those labelled 1 should be taught before those labelled 2, and so on. In this way, children's understanding can develop in a logical way: nouns before noun phrases and verbs before verb tenses and adverbs, for example. The objectives in white are the age-related expectations for Year 4. Those in grey detail the key skills that need consolidating before more advanced concepts are introduced (or alongside their introduction, in some cases). There are also several grey objectives (such as 9a) which have been added because they are part and parcel of good writing for this age group but don't feature in the National Curriculum.

Year 4 writing – Steps in Learning					
Spelling		I can follow the Y3 spelling rules and spell most of the words on the Y3/4 word list			
	1	I can use further prefixes and suffixes and understand how to add them (e.g. il-, im-, -ir/-ous, -tion)			
	2	I can spell further homophones (e.g. threw/through, meet/meat, wait/weight)			
	3	I can spell words that are often misspelt from the Y3/4 word list (e.g. separate, library, to/two/too, a lot, their/there)			
	4	I can use the first two or three letters of a word to check its spelling in a dictionary			
	5	I can write from memory simple sentences including words and punctuation taught so far			
H	6	I understand which letters are best left unjoined (e.g. capital letters to any other letter, z)			
	7	I can improve the quality of my handwriting (e.g. letters consistent in size, ascenders and descenders not touching)			
Composition	8	I can plan to use the correct structure in my writing, adapting form and style			
		I can open and/or end writing appropriately			
	9	I can use increasingly varied vocabulary and grammar			
		I can use a variety of stylistic features for purpose and effect (e.g. alliteration, simile, metaphors, personification)			

Figure 7 Steps in Learning for writing in Year 4

		I can use techniques to engage the reader (e.g. build tension, opinion, rhetorical questions)			
	10	I can organise paragraphs around a theme, linking them when appropriate (e.g. topic sentences)			
		I can change paragraph with increasing accuracy (e.g. 3 Ps (person/place/point) and a T (time))			
	11	I can create settings, characters and plot in stories			
	12	I can write non-fiction, using simple devices to organise my work (e.g. headings and subheadings, bullet points)			
	13	I can evaluate and edit, learning from the effectiveness of my own and others' writing and making improvements			
	14	I can evaluate and edit, improving my writing by making changes to grammar and vocabulary			
	15	I can proofread for spelling and punctuation			
	16	I can read my own writing to a group or class using appropriate intonation/tone/volume so that the meaning is clear			

Vocabulary, Grammar and Punctuation		I understand, and use, **1** nouns, **2** verbs, **1** adjectives, **1** pronouns, **2** conjunctions, **4** adverbs and **4** prepositions appropriately			
	17	**1** I can choose nouns or pronouns to make my meaning clear and avoid repetition (e.g. Sam unwrapped his snack and picked up the bug. It tasted great!)			
		1 I can recognise and use collective nouns appropriately (e.g. swarm of bees, flight of stairs)			
		1 I can use the determiners **a**, **an** and **the** appropriately (e.g. a crazy idea, an iceberg, the sun) and recognise numbers as determiners			
		1 I can use a wide range of punctuation accurately and consistently (e.g. question marks, exclamation marks, commas in lists, inverted commas)			
	18	**2** I can use a wider range of conjunctions to extend a range of sentences with more than one clause			
		2 I can identify main and subordinate clauses accurately and consistently (e.g. It had been a fantastic day even though we got wet through.)			
		2 I can use powerful verbs to describe (e.g. the man collapsed instead of the man fell suddenly)			
		2 I can make the appropriate tense choices for a task (e.g. simple past, past progressive, present perfect for narrative)			

Figure 7 (Continued)

	3 I know and follow the rules of Standard English (subject-verb agreement, consistency of tense, avoidance of slang, avoidance of double negatives)			
19	**3** I can use the apostrophe for contraction and possession (including regular and irregular plural nouns) (e.g. Jessica's book/the children's hobby)			
20	**3** I can punctuate direct speech using inverted commas and other punctuation (e.g. comma after the reporting clause, end punctuation within inverted commas)			
21	**4** I can use fronted adverbials followed by commas (e.g. Later that day,… (when)/At the end of the road,… (where)/With great care,… (how))			
22	**4** I recognise the difference between a clause and a phrase and use both appropriately (e.g. At midnight,… /When the clock struck midnight,…)			
23	**4** I can use conjunctions, adverbs or prepositions to express time, place and cause (e.g. I'd never been before. (a)/She ate before she went out. (c)/He washed before tea. (p))			
	4 I can use expanded noun phrases with modifying adjectives and prepositional phrases (e.g. … in an isolated cottage at the top of the hill.)			

Grammar sequence

1. nouns (including proper nouns) and basic sentence punctuation (including statements, questions, exclamations and commands), noun phrases and pronouns to replace nouns and noun phrases
2. verbs, clauses and connecting clauses using conjunctions, revision of verb tenses – simple, progressive and present perfect
3. rules of Standard English, apostrophes and direct speech punctuation
4. adverbs, adverbials and fronted adverbials (including the difference between a phrase and a clause), using conjunctions, adverbs or prepositions to express time, place and cause

Figure 7 (Continued)

The grammar sequence shown underneath the table gives teachers an at-a-glance guide to key concepts in that year group and where they fit within a logical progression. If adopted as a whole-school approach, you would see each year group beginning the autumn term with teaching and learning focused on nouns and basic sentence construction before moving on to noun phrases, and so on. There would be a culture of consolidation in which children are given the opportunity to revisit key concepts in each year group; to transfer knowledge from working to long-term memory. The stronger the children's grasp of these concepts, the lighter touch the teaching. In this way, more children are able to build their knowledge and understanding of new concepts onto prior learning. Also, teachers could identify children who are experiencing difficulties with underpinning skills and can agree targets accordingly.

Children's target areas can be shared with children (at the front of their writing books, perhaps) on a table of their age-related expectations (Figure 8) or, if their needs lie outside the age-related expectations, handwritten onto a priority targets template (Figure 9). At my own school, a child's current target, whether an age-related expectation or priority target, is identified with the date it was agreed written into the left-hand box and highlighted in one colour. In the right-hand boxes, dates on which the child has made progress by using the focus skill independently and to good effect in their writing are noted and, when three or more such dates have been earned, the right and left-hand boxes are highlighted in a different colour. In this way, teachers can keep a check on how long it is taking children to achieve specific targets and, if necessary, talk to them about whether they need more help. Also, children have a visual reminder of how they are getting on as a writer.

Ideas in practice

Name: Rachel Draper
Teaching level: Year 2
School: Sacred Heart Catholic Primary

This year I have begun to use the Steps in Learning document for Year 2 as a long-term plan for English. For one unit, we used *The Lighthouse Keeper's Tea* by Ronda and David Armitage. The children loved the story. We built a picture of a lighthouse by watching video clips featuring lighthouses and focused on hearing the sights and sounds. We used the text to prompt a sequence of lessons on verbs with the aim of preparing the children to write a diary entry as the main character in the book, and use their knowledge of verbs in their final piece of writing.

We did lots of work around verbs – spotting and highlighting them within the text, role-playing verbs in action and then practising writing sentences about particular actions accurately. We then transferred this knowledge to writing in context. I used modelling to guide the children's work and there was lots of discussion around their first efforts. The children got plenty of opportunities to practise before writing their final independent piece. I could really see the progress the children made over the two weeks.

I continued to consolidate verb knowledge in the next unit and the children were soon ready to take the next step and look at the role of verbs in each clause and at joining clauses using conjunctions. As well as using great quality texts, having the logical skills sequence to teach from has brought my English teaching to life. It has helped me to make sense of the curriculum and to really home in on the needs of my children. When we're ready to move on, I know exactly where I need to go next with my teaching and I can really see that the children are reaping the rewards.

Things to think about

- Where are the majority of children in your class up to according to the grammar progression at the foot of the Steps in Learning document for your year group (Appendix 2)?
- What underpinning skills do your pupils need in order to make maximum progress against the next age-related expectation you plan to teach? How can the Steps in Learning help you to plan your next unit?

Stage 4 writing targets					
Spelling	1	I can use further prefixes and suffixes and understand how to add them (e.g. il-, im-, -ir/ -ous, -tion)			
	2	I can spell further homophones (e.g. threw/through, meet/meat, wait/weight)			
	3	I can spell words that are often misspelt from the Y3/4 word list (e.g. separate, library, to/two/too, a lot, their/there)			
	4	I can use the first two or three letters of a word to check its spelling in a dictionary			
	5	I can write from memory simple sentences including words and punctuation taught so far			
H	6	I understand which letters are best left unjoined (e.g. capital letters to any other letter, z)			
	7	I can improve the quality of my handwriting (e.g. letters consistent in size, ascenders and descenders not touching)			
Composition	8	I can plan to use the correct structure in my writing, adapting form and style			
	9	I can use increasingly varied vocabulary and grammar			
	10	I can organise paragraphs around a theme, linking them when appropriate			
	11	I can create (a) settings, (b) characters and (c) plot in stories			
	12	I can write non-fiction, using simple devices to organise my work (e.g. headings and subheadings, bullet points)			
	13	I can evaluate and edit, learning from the effectiveness of my own and others' writing and making improvements			
	14	I can evaluate and edit, improving my writing by making changes to grammar and vocabulary			
	15	I can proofread for spelling and punctuation			
	16	I can read my own writing to a group or class using appropriate intonation/tone/volume so that the meaning is clear			

Figure 8 Year 4 children's writing target sheet

Vocabulary, Grammar and Punctuation					
	17	I can choose nouns or pronouns to make my meaning clear and avoid repetition (e.g. Sam unwrapped his snack and picked up the bug. It tasted great!)			
	18	I can use a wider range of conjunctions to extend a range of sentences with more than one clause			
	19	I can use the apostrophe for (a) contraction and (b) possession (including regular and irregular plural nouns) (e.g. Jessica's book/the children's hobby)			
	20	I can punctuate direct speech using inverted commas and other punctuation (e.g. comma after the reporting clause, end punctuation within inverted commas)			
	21	I can use fronted adverbials followed by commas (e.g. Later that day,… (when)/At the end of the road,… (where)/With great care,… (how))			
	22	I recognise the difference between a clause and a phrase and use both appropriately (e.g. At midnight,… /When the clock struck midnight,…)			
	23	I can use conjunctions, adverbs or prepositions to express time, place and cause (e.g. I'd never been before. (a)/She ate before she going out. (c)/He washed before tea. (p))			
	24	I can understand and use the stage 4 grammatical vocabulary			

Figure 8 (Continued)

	1				
	2				
	3				
	4				
	5				
	6				
	7				
	8				

Figure 9 Priority target template

Reflection points

- Do you reflect on what your school is doing to encourage children to read for pleasure every year? The more children read, the more likely they are to make rapid progress in their English skills.
- Is your focus on writing for purpose when helping your pupils develop key skills for writing?
- Do you recognise that to best equip children with the skills they need to say something in writing, you should first to get children wanting to write, give them something to say and a reason for saying it? (This idea will be explored further in Chapter 4.)
- Do you recognise that, to help children maximise their progress as writers, routine consolidation and systematic progression needs to be built into phonics, spelling and grammar teaching?
- Can you see a role for Steps in Learning to help ensure that you are planning from the bigger picture of the skills that constitute effective writing in your year group? Can you see the benefit of enabling children to acquire skills in a logical order and spend time practising the steps that lead to understanding of ARE?

3
Talk and thought

To reach and go beyond their age-related expectations for writing, today's primary school child has to be productive. He has to be productive physically, using and applying new and existing skills daily in his writing, and he needs to be productive mentally so that he can show his understanding, or lack of it, on a regular basis and become more self-reliant by doing more thinking for himself. For children to learn more deeply, they have to think more deeply.

In this chapter, we will discover that talk is an essential vehicle for children's thinking. We will consider how *thinking* and *talking* can be used to enhance *writing* outcomes. In fact, we will explore ways of using English lessons to create opportunities for each of these three important disciplines to support and enhance the other.

One of the key goals of this book is to offer a systematic way of planning. We need to stop trying to reinvent the wheel every time we plan for English. What if we could put our faith in a simple, user-friendly routine for planning that pulls together essential strands of teaching and learning? Figure 10 shows a planning pyramid that will guide us in such a routine, which we will explore in detail in Chapter 6. We have already established the importance of allowing key **skills** to drive our thinking when planning a unit of English – hence its place at the top of the pyramid. How exactly do we want our pupils' understanding and writing to improve during this current unit? Next, we need to consider the context in which the children will work. What will the **writing outcome(s)** be and what **talk and thought** will help to pave the way to this writing?

Creating opportunities for thinking, particularly opportunities in which ideas can be discovered, shared and refined through collaboration, should be central to our practice as we work towards quality writing outcomes. Let's find out how this might work.

There's group work and there's group work

Children working together in groups is common practice in primary schools and has been since the 1970s. The Bullock report (1975) pointed out that, in the primary years especially, a child's ability to speak and listen is nearly always more developed than their ability to read and write. Sharing their work with others through talk can benefit children by helping them to develop their thinking in any curriculum area. Examples of such 'sharing' might include guided work, pooling information, jointly creating a document or a poster, or discussing a group problem or question.

Researchers such as Slavin (2009) and Vass and Littleton (2010) have concluded that collaboration is a powerful aid to study and useful for the development of reasoning. However, research has also shown that in most classrooms, much of the time, group work is quite unproductive (Littleton and Howe 2010) and of

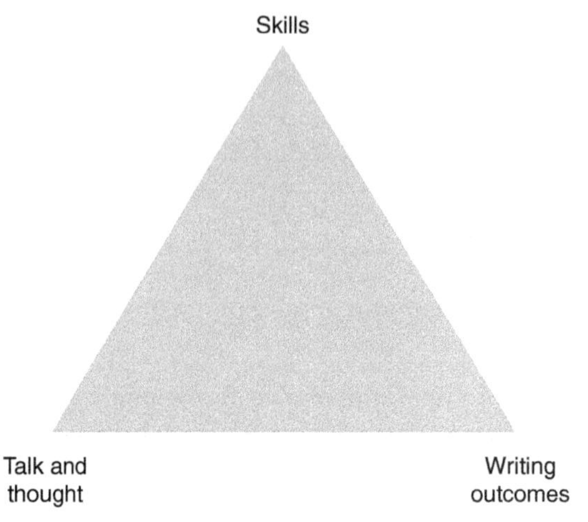

Figure 10 The planning pyramid for English

little educational value. Often children interact in a quarrelsome manner, and some group members don't participate while others dominate.

So grouping children as an organisational strategy for teaching and learning may be common, but its effectiveness for promoting understanding and thinking cannot be taken for granted. In their book, *Interthinking: Putting Talk to Work*, Karen Littleton and Neil Mercer say that many students, perhaps most, don't know how to talk and work together effectively, but teachers assume that they do. They need to be taught how to do so and just giving them opportunities to collaborate is not enough.

The Open University's Thinking Together research focused on talk that occurs as school children work together in groups and established that unless children understand precisely what we (as teachers) mean when we ask them to discuss their work, their talk together may not allow an interchange of ideas and opinions. It seems that, although children in classroom groups talk with one another, they often do so 'without any prolonged thinking about ideas, reasons, evidence or information. There seems to be a low natural incidence of the kind of discussion which has been called "Exploratory Talk", a way of using language for reasoning' (Lyn Dawes and Claire Sams, 2004).

Dawes and Sams point out that the capacity to collaborate is not an innate quality but it can be developed through a variety of experiences and enhanced by direct teaching and learning in classroom situations. Why? What is so desirable about ensuring children have the ability to collaborate effectively: to use talk to reason together?

In their research, Littleton and Mercer found that teachers could teach children how to use Exploratory talk, and that increasing its use in primary classrooms could significantly improve attainment for the children involved. In one study involving seven classes of nine- to ten-year-olds, children were guided in effective ways of working in groups before they embarked on a sequence of mathematics and science lessons over a period of eight months. The teaching approach emphasised classroom discussion, group work and the development of children's awareness of talking for learning. Children in target classes and control classes were given SATs-based tests before and after the intervention period. The pre/post SATs scores showed a significantly higher improvement for children in target classes than those in the control classes, and target classes also showed significantly greater improvements in non-verbal reasoning.

Why should children learn to collaborate?

Beyond primary school, doesn't educational success require considerably more than learning and using facts and skills? It requires the ability to justify opinions, analyses, solutions and conclusions. So too do many roles in the world of work. Occupations that require the planning and solving of problems as a team are as common today as they ever have been. We only have to look at advertisements for jobs as varied as salesperson, hotel manager, researcher or accounting assistant to see how commonly they seek people who are 'good at working in a team and possess excellent interpersonal skills'. Even in occupations not normally associated with language use, we find that talk amongst groups of people has a crucial role in getting things done. An awful lot of talk, for example, is required between architects, builders and other skilled workers to turn plans for a new building into a reality on the ground. For this to happen, all concerned need a common conception of their goal, some shared values and, crucially, a shared language for addressing technical aspects of the job and finding solutions to problems encountered along the way.

If we define reasoning as the process of thinking about something in a logical way in order to reach a decision/form a conclusion or judgement, then surely the more teachers can do to develop reasoning skills, the better. What Neil Mercer, Lyn Dawes and their peers have found is that the best way to do this is through talk – through collaboration – but not just any collaboration. Three things need to be in place for classroom collaboration to be successful:

- the children need to be absolutely clear on their common goal
- there need to be rules governing the talk so that all participants know exactly what is expected of them
- children need the language skills to enable them to articulate their ideas and to deepen thinking amongst the group.

The introduction of a rigid curriculum in recent years and an emphasis on 'standards' and assessment have meant that the space and time for learning conversations has diminished. Part of the challenge for teachers looking to develop reasoning skills through English is to prioritise the teaching of speaking and listening skills to give them the shared language they need to reach common goals in the classroom.

Thinking through talk

Using language to make sense of the world is something that comes naturally to us. Young children do this when they play together. They take on the role of Mum, Dad or teacher to explore different situations and learn from each other as they do so. Also, imagine yourself on a CPD training course. If the course leader asks you to take some time to think about a teaching point, don't you almost immediately turn to the person next to you to ask what they think? Their response and the ensuing conversation helps us to form opinions, develops our own thinking and often raises further questions. It is likely that the resulting understanding goes beyond what would have been achieved if you and the other delegates had kept your thoughts to yourselves.

Neil Mercer (2013) uses the idea of the 'social brain' in explaining our ability as human beings to link our individual minds to create a powerful problem-solving tool. He argues that this ability played a major role in the evolution of our species. Mercer developed a dialogue-based thinking and learning approach, called 'Thinking together', to harness this power in the classroom. Thinking together is based on over two decades of classroom-based research which informed the UK National Curriculum guidance. The approach puts great store in giving clear focus for children's class discussions through an agreed set of ground rules, and organising children in groups of three to use Exploratory talk as they work on curriculum-based activities.

For me, there are three big ways of getting children to engage in powerful thinking through talk:

- Exploratory talk
- Philosophy for children
- Drama.

We will now consider how each of these talk formats can be used as powerful precursors to writing.

Exploratory talk

Using Exploratory talk, children learn not merely to interact but to 'interthink', and teachers' planning incorporates the development of children's thinking and communication skills into curriculum learning.

First identified by the pioneering British educational researcher Douglas Barnes, Exploratory talk invites participants to engage critically but constructively with each other's ideas in a discussion on a given question. Relevant knowledge is shared and suggestions and opinions are actively sought through questioning and challenge. All contributions are treated with respect. According to Mercer, Exploratory talk is the perfect vehicle for reasoning: you certainly witness reasoning in action through the use of words like 'I think…', 'because…' and 'why…?'. With its emphasis on knowledge sharing and a commitment to a shared goal, it is exactly the sort of interaction that can be witnessed in fields like science, law and business every day. Such is its power that, according to Dawes and Sams (2004), it is 'reasonable to expect that education should help every child to become aware of its value and become able to use it effectively'.

It may well be reasonable but, as Dawes and Sams point out, it is very unusual for children to be given direct teaching which helps them to work and, more specifically, talk together productively with other children. Such teaching is necessary not only because of the tremendous rewards that Exploratory talk offers but also because children come into our schools and our classrooms with such different experiences of talk from home. Some children are lucky enough to collaborate well together and may have had experiences at home in which they are asked for their opinions and contribute to discussions of an exploratory kind. Others are not so lucky, with limited experience of talk of any depth, and may struggle without clear guidance from their teacher.

Ground rules

Unless children understand precisely what is expected of them in collaborative tasks, the talk will be unproductive. In the Thinking together approach, the teacher and the class agree on a set of ground rules. The children reflect on what they think will make a good discussion and their involvement in formulating the rules builds ownership. Clearly these rules will vary depending on the age of the children but they may look something like these:

- We will share our ideas with each other
- We will ask everyone to say what they think

- We will give reasons for our ideas
- We will listen to everyone and respect each other's opinions
- When we disagree, we will ask 'why' and explain our opinions
- When everyone has said all they want, we will think about what to do together
- We will try to reach an agreement.

With the last point, it doesn't matter if there is no consensus of opinion or an agreement reached. What matters is that 'contrasting opinions' and 'seeking agreement' are features of the discussions children have because this means that the children are engaged in collective reasoning. Howe (2009, 2010) suggests that having to seek agreement encourages children to pursue their discussions in more depth and to more certain conclusions.

Organising children in mixed-ability groups of three is recommended. I have personally found this to be successful in my own teaching, especially with children who are more reluctant to speak in a larger group. Assigning specific roles like spokesperson (with responsibility for feeding back to the class), involver (making sure everyone contributes) and why police (making sure everyone gives reasons for the opinions and ideas) can also help to focus attention to the task.

The importance of enabling children to collaborate is huge. They literally do think together. They enjoy being a valued part of an active discussion and can really gain confidence in their own voice. The ground rules give children a break from the normal classroom dynamic. Children don't have to compete too hard for attention or have to be constantly on their guard about revealing their thoughts and feelings for fear of being criticised or ignored. Thinking together researchers found that under-achieving pupils benefitted most from consistent use of the ground rules in a structured dialogue, and children with a range of special needs became better integrated into the class and gained in confidence through working in mixed ability groups of three.

Before children take part in their first Exploratory talk, it can be very helpful to explicitly teach them speaking and listening skills, such as listening and responding to others, asking relevant questions and challenging with respect. Teachers can provide contexts for collaboration in which they can apply such skills, clearly setting out aims at the outset, getting involved to draw attention to different contributions made or taking the talk in a slightly different direction. They can also reflect on the quality of the talk at the end. This is not an add-on to the curriculum but part and parcel of the teaching and learning in curriculum subjects like science, history and English.

Exploring themes and ideas in shared texts in English can provide a perfect context for this collaborative thinking. How often do we skirt over the deeper meanings that lie behind many quality texts because our focus is on setting description or the author's use of expanded noun phrases, or simply because we want to get through the novel? Asking the right question or questions around these deeper meanings can provide wonderful opportunities, not only for children to get full enjoyment from a text but to think more deeply through collaboration. Deeper thinking about matters that engage children in this way can really enrich the writing outcomes that follow.

Firstly, focus on the big ideas behind a story or text. For example, the picture book *Leon and the Place Between*, by Angela McAllister and Grahame Baker-Smith, is a beautifully-illustrated picture book story of a young boy called Leon who visits a circus with his family. They are captivated by a show by the amazing Abdul Kazam and Leon gets swept up in the magic after stepping forward as a volunteer. The book has strong themes of magic and believing: themes that are very relevant to the lives of young children.

There is a tremendous opportunity here to unlock a treasure trove of ideas which will have children bursting to write. Take your time to form the right question for children to discuss. Ideally, you want this to divide opinion and open the door to the contrasting ideas that will generate reasoning in practice.

When the book was used recently with a Year 2 class I know, the teacher simply posed the question 'What is magic?'. This allowed some children to suggest that magic is the domain of true professionals who recognise and respect its power for good or bad. Others enthused about the work of the Tooth Fairy, Santa Claus, and alike. The teacher went on to channel some of the children's ideas into a letter written in role as Leon. The letter sought to convince Leon's sceptical brother, Billy, of the existence of magic; giving children the opportunity to use question marks and exclamation marks to good effect.

Exploratory talk is most useful when the teacher wants to set a clear direction for a class discussion so that it leads naturally into a writing task. It is just as useful in response to a non-fiction stimulus as it is to fiction. Take bees, for example. Now there's an opportunity for some big ideas. On a recent writing course I ran for primary teachers, we took a detailed look at *The Book of Bees* by Piotr Socha. With a Year 3 unit of learning in mind and research on the pros and cons of bees from the book under our belts, we took part in an Exploratory talk addressing the question 'What would life be like without bees?'. The talk spanned everything, from an end to bee stings through the loss of a beautiful creature, to a serious threat to mankind due to the loss of food-producing plants like apple and onion, as well as the creatures that feed on those plants and so on up the food chain, and the current decline in bee populations. All sorts of writing opportunities – directly and indirectly influenced by the talk – were discussed including an explanation of the importance of bees, a 'Save Our Bees' campaign and links to the pollination of plants in science.

Ideas in practice

Name: Rebecca Taylor
Teaching level: Year 4
School: St Williams Catholic Primary

I am encouraging children to talk more in the English lessons that I teach. Through using Exploratory talk children are now more familiar with sharing ideas and these ideas develop more and more. They are now encouraging each other to 'think outside the box'.

For example, when using direct speech as the skill driver and the book *The Tear Thief* by Carol Ann Duffy and Nicoletta Ceccoli, we had some really positive whole-class and small group discussions around different tears and the reasons behind why people cry. My specific Exploratory talk question was 'Is the Tear Thief a good character or not?'. The children explored the word 'thief' and the connotations with this word. I asked the question before reading the book and after reading to see if our opinion changed at all. This is something that I have not had in my lessons until now. The talk that the children had really developed their thinking and allowed them to come up with alternative suggestions for a character much more confidently than before. The children have written newspaper articles reporting a sighting of the Tear Thief with quotes to show direct speech. This idea came from the children themselves, which I think truly shows that they are wanting to write rather than being told what to write.

We then designed an alternative character to the Tear Thief and they talked around different possibilities much more confidently than before. The children wrote a story featuring this character, and applied their knowledge of direct speech. The children are noting that the skills are not genre-specific and are transferrable which is having an incredible impact on the progress that they are making. Due to the fact that the children have been talking more, they are more familiar with sharing ideas and using Exploratory talk is developing their thinking skills. Because of this, and the fact that the children are taking ownership of their skills development, the writing that I am now marking is of much higher quality and the progress that the children are making really shows as the children are truly engaged and a part of their own learning.

Things to think about

- Do any of the texts you are using with your class offer big ideas that could fuel Exploratory talk?
- Do your children ever get the opportunity to choose the form of writing that gives them a vehicle for what they have to say?

Such talk also gives teachers the perfect opportunity to model, highlight or explain language that will help them to articulate their thinking and build more detailed paragraphs in their non-fiction writing. This is something a lot of primary-aged children find difficult. They can happily make a series of points in their writing but often the explanation or evidence behind those points is missing. A reader needs this detail to really make sense of what a writer is trying to say and children stand a far better chance of including such detail if they have done the deeper thinking first. If words like 'for example…','even though…' and 'on the other hand…' are emphasised and explained in the right talk contexts, then children will understand how to use such reasoning vocabulary to build their ideas in writing.

Also, teachers in England need look no further than Exploratory talk to meet the oracy requirements of the National Curriculum. The vast majority of objectives for Years 1 to 6 – including articulating and justifying answers, arguments and opinions, asking relevant questions to extend understanding and knowledge, and developing understanding through speculating, hypothesising, imagining and exploring ideas – are very much at home in structured, collaborative talk.

In Chapter 4, we will focus in more detail on engaging children in their learning. Sometimes, this is about working with a stimulus that comes from the children, as in this case study.

Ideas in practice

Name: Janet Dean
Teaching level: Year 4
School: Platt Bridge Community Primary

In my current class, the children have poor language skills and use of vocabulary, which severely impacts upon their spoken and written work.

I began by selecting a topic which the children could initially discuss (Superheroes), as from previous experience I knew that writing has to come from the children's interests which motivate and enthuse them. In other writing units, I had discussed the text, vocabulary, etc., as is usual classroom practice. Talk and debate has been a part of my teaching but hasn't achieved the effective writing from my children that was expected from them. I planned my writing unit thinking specifically 'how' talk in the classroom would be constructive and allow all my children to fully participate. I have some children who will listen but do not contribute actively to the group, which usually ends up with myself leading the discussion. Whilst this in itself isn't a bad thing as I have to clarify, demonstrate and model, it didn't produce thinkers, language rich pupils and independent talkers.

My first session was totally dedicated to talking. I had chosen visual stimuli as a way to engage them as I wanted to generate ideas/vocabulary to collect. In my target group, I discussed the 'rules' of talking in a group and then waited, (usually I would ask a question or lead them). Initially, they were keen to talk about the pictures, their experiences, films and books, etc. but listening to the discussion, I quickly realised that the 'talk' was actually not producing anything of substance. I intervened and redirected the discussion. Through open-ended questioning, paraphrasing, probing and asking children to fully explain their understanding of what they said and language used, we eventually collected some lovely ideas, a word bank of adjectives that were suitable and appropriate, and ultimately, what the children had generated themselves.

My next session also incorporated lots of talk. This time, we looked at a variety of texts with grammatical features I wished the children to use in their writing. This time, I didn't rush the process. I gave the children time to discuss the grammar and vocabulary and the skill of the author, bringing in purpose and audience, something my children really struggled with. As a group we were able to explore words, their meaning, synonyms and use in sentences, orally rehearse sentences and 'play' with them to get the right one they wanted. It was a really positive session. I felt the children really benefited from the time to talk and discuss the grammar, vocabulary, skills from authors and, also, being able to think through what they wanted to say and write.

The writing they produced for their Superhero stories was much improved. The 'talk' proved to be instrumental in supporting the children's writing. They made connections through seeing how authors used language, vocabulary and, through exploration, were able to write sentences that included the skills and correct use of vocabulary and grammatical features I wanted.

My target group now lead their own discussions, are much more confident at speaking and orally rehearsing sentences and willing to explore and delve into a text. The key for me is allowing the time to talk and not rushing the process in our very busy classrooms.

Things to think about

- Are there planned opportunities for children to develop speaking and listening skills in your school time or is such development accidental?
- Do you provide enough opportunities in class for children to talk and think about their ideas before they write?

Philosophy for children

Philosophy for children (P4C) is another excellent model for collaborative thinking. It is a wonderful way of bringing teachers and children together to discuss things that matter. A range of different stimuli can be used including music, pictures, pieces of film or stories – picture story books being particularly useful. These can be used to prompt philosophical dialogues. Like Exploratory talk, P4C is enquiry-based learning that involves children exploring big concepts such as friendship, fairness or happiness. Its aim is to help children become more willing and able to ask questions, construct arguments and engage in reasoned discussion.

One approach involves teaching children how to create their own philosophical questions and then choosing a question as the focus for the enquiry or dialogue that will prompt a rich exchange of ideas and differences of opinion. However, it can work just as well (particularly if you are constrained by time) if the teacher chooses the question in order to lead the enquiry in a particular direction. 'Is it ever OK to lie?', for example, would be an excellent question if it reflected the events in a shared story. The teacher, as facilitator, can intervene where appropriate to ensure curriculum integration and, crucially, support the children in their thinking, reasoning and questioning, as well as the way the children speak and listen to each other in the dialogue.

Benefits of P4C

Research into the impact of Philosophy for children is limited. However, a 2013 study commissioned by the Education Endowment Fund involving 48 primary schools across England found that regular P4C sessions over the course of a year had a positive impact on Key Stage 2 outcomes in reading and mathematics, particularly for children eligible for free school meals. This is significant because the P4C was not explicitly focused on improving Key Stage 2 outcomes. Feedback from teachers and pupils also suggested that P4C had a beneficial impact on wider outcomes such as pupils' confidence to speak, patience when listening to others, and self-esteem. Some teachers also reported a positive impact on general classroom engagement.

In an earlier study, 105 children in the last two years of primary school were regularly taught philosophical, enquiry-based lessons and showed significant improvements on tests of their verbal, numerical and spatial abilities at the end of the 16-month period. Unusually, the children were retested two years later and the benefits appeared to have persisted, whereas the scores of control group children deteriorated from their inferior scores two years earlier (Topping and Trickey, 2007). Children learn through P4C that their ideas have value and the ideas of other children have value too. Another huge benefit is that, through reading, thinking, and talking about issues emerging from story books, children establish a stronger text-to-life connection. This can change their perspective on their studies, helping them to more closely relate their English learning to their everyday lives instead of seeing it as just another required subject.

Ideas in practice

Name: Sarah Platt
Teaching level: Year 6
School: Queen's Park Primary

Following the terrorist attacks in Manchester and London, in the summer of 2017, I found that some children in my class wanted to talk about them. I felt I needed to give them a way of talking about some of the wider issues involved, hoping that perhaps we could get something positive out of it. I decided to use the picture book *The Pirates Next Door* by Jonny Duddle as a stimulus for a P4C session.

The story is about a family of pirates who move in to a seaside town, next door to a little girl. The girl was delighted. She had been wishing for a friend to play with, but the rest of the town reacted differently. They complained about the noise the pirates made, their uncleanliness and the fact that they were digging holes everywhere, and they sent a petition to the council to get rid of them. They eventually got their wish, only to find after the pirates had gone that they had left some buried treasure in each residents' garden. Suddenly, when it was too late, the residents began to see the positives about their temporary neighbours.

The children enjoyed the story but enjoyed discussing the meanings behind it even more. The question they chose to discuss was 'Can you judge a book by its cover?'. Initially, we talked literally about books and the children decided that you could form a first impression of what some books were going to be like before reading them: the cover suggesting that it was going to be a funny story or an adventure. But that you couldn't form a proper opinion about it until you had read it. The issue of prejudice soon came up and was discussed at length – in relation to the pirates in the story, then traveller families and then people from ethnic minorities in wider western society.

Adolf Hitler and Martin Luther King, who the children had learnt about previously, both came into the discussion and the children became really passionate in their defence of people who were somehow different. They were aware of prejudice in the wider community and some got quite annoyed that some human beings could be treated differently, just because of the way they look or the community they belong to. As a result of my intervention, the discussion ended with some thoughts on how we need to treat all people with respect in our own lives.

In a subsequent lesson, the children worked in threes, and then larger groups, to develop ideas for a sequel to *The Pirates Next Door*. I was amazed by the quality of the ideas. One group decided that the Matilda, the little girl that wanted a playmate, went on an adventure on the high seas when the pirates returned and was taken to the island they called home, only to suffer prejudice herself at the hands of the island's pirate residents. Another group had the same seaside town visited by a circus. The residents hadn't fully learnt their lesson, though, and began to complain about their traveller visitors – until they were all treated to a free performance that left them in awe.

The children chose which version of the sequel they wanted to write and planned with a like-minded group. The writing I got was fabulous and all thanks to a P4C session and a picture book that touched a nerve.

Things to think about

- Is there room in your curriculum to give children a voice, through P4C, on big issues such as those in current affairs?
- Can you see how rich dialogue about issues that relate to children's lives can lead to children writing from the heart?

Drama into writing

Drama can be another incredibly powerful route into writing, especially if children are given some autonomy in deciding where the drama goes. It is another way for children to 'think together' through talk and allows them to engage deeply in a scenario (perhaps prompted by a text), and understand it better.

It is only by dwelling in themes that meaning can be understood (Polanyi, 1967). If we can get beyond children feeling self-conscious in front of their classmates, such deep engagement can also mean that the drama is sustained through the actual act of writing, resulting in increased concentration and commitment.

What the research says

A number of research studies (e.g. Barrs and Cork, 2001) have found that when drama is integrated into the teaching of reading, writing, speaking and listening, the quality of related writing is enhanced, particularly when it is written in role. Bearne et al. (2004) also found that using drama increased independence and reduced the need for adult support during writing.

Teresa Cremin et al. (2006) involved two classes of ten- to 11-year-olds and one class of six- to seven-year-olds in a year-long research project which examined the relationship between drama and writing in South East England. They found that, when children had been involved in drama, the children found writing easier. As part of the process of creating and inhabiting fictional worlds, the children built belief and deepened their involvement in the narrative. Writing in role from a particular stance developed during the drama appeared to strengthen their writing. The convictions that the children developed through drama were often retained in their writing, so the writer's point of view was expressed clearly. The context had personal significance for the children and so their motivation to write increased, and the drama provided audience and purpose for the children's written communications. It also prompted powerful thoughts, feelings and information which were harnessed in writing.

In one lesson, inspired by David Bennett and Karin Littlewood's book *The Lonely Whale*, the six- to seven-year-olds took up the roles as sailors who were shipwrecked and rescued by a whale. During the role play, the sailors built shelters and looked for food before finding the whale beached. The sailors were divided as to whether to help the whale: the captain blamed the whale for their misfortune but many totally disagreed, telling the captain he was being unfair and that it was his fault they were shipwrecked in the first place. With no solution in sight, the teacher decided to capitalise on the children's involvement and the tension generated, and seized the moment to write.

'The class settled quickly, producing messages for bottles, posters requesting help. The majority wrote with focused intent, many even remained standing. The situation had provided both an immediate purpose and an "intrinsic need" to write' (Cremin et al., 2006). One child, Annalise, asked for urgent help to rescue the whale, her best friend and only transport home, as time was running out. Her plea reflected the sense of panic and tension experienced in the classroom. In both the drama and in her writing, Annalise adopted the role of a concerned sailor and this perspective enabled her to express her sense of injustice and voice her worries about returning safely home.

Seizing the moment to write

Cremin and her colleagues urge teachers to adopt this 'seize the moment' approach to writing through drama, remaining open to possibilities. The drama offers children the support they need and has the capacity to foster thoughtful, imaginative and effective writing. 'To offer young writers the supportive scaffold of drama, teachers need to involve children in often conflict-driven, open-ended contexts and adroitly seize moment/s for writing, allowing the learners considerable choice in terms of perspective, purpose and form'.

The idea of harnessing children's imagination to produce writing through drama is a fascinating one. I have long been amazed at children's ability to suspend reality and immerse themselves into a fictional world. The Year 6 children I took to participate in 'A Victorian Christmas' at Croxteth Hall, in Liverpool, for a number of years would thoroughly enjoy becoming maids, woodcutters, footmen and alike to prepare for Christmas for Lord and Lady Sefton. The children were well aware that their 'work' was make-believe, that the real world continued to exist around them, but for a few precious hours they really felt what it was like to be in domestic service in the late 19th century. We have discussed the huge value of using children's own experiences to prompt authentic writing. Those experiences are no less valuable educationally if they take place in a fictional world.

This fact is the basis of the teaching approach known as Mantle of the Expert. Developed by drama teacher Dorothy Heathcote (1994), the approach sees children taking on roles as experts in an imaginary enterprise. The children know that it is make-believe and that they are not really experts but are tasked to work together as the team responsible for getting a particular job done. Along the way, they encounter problems, or tensions. These either arise naturally or are pre-planned and introduced by the teacher, and are essential to adding complexity, keeping the drama interesting and creating new opportunities for learning and writing.

Like Exploratory talk, this is an inquiry-based approach that puts children right at the centre of their learning. It involves a genuine commitment from teachers to work collaboratively with their pupils and requires a belief that children have something significant to offer – their ideas, knowledge and skills. Children are encouraged to explore multiple perspectives on the issue at hand. Again, they listen to different points of view, explore alternatives and use their reasoning skills to find a way forward. It is important and relevant to them because they are involved in the decisions and share a responsibility for what happens in this imaginary world.

The teacher and children drift between the imaginary world and the real world, in which the children might need further information, get advice from their teacher or do some research if the scenario is linked to studies in another subject area. The beauty is that the teacher can 'seize the moment' to write whenever she, or the children, feel is appropriate.

In one example shared online by Tim Taylor and Dr Brian Edmiston, a teacher or TA pretends to be an injured mountaineer, stranded on a mountainside in treacherous conditions. The children are gradually enlisted into the drama-inquiry as members of a mountain rescue team, with the aim of writing a shared story. Along the way, they are asked to produce a plan of action, see the events through the eyes of a reporter, shift back in time to the first aid training they will need to call upon, split up into a medical team and a rescue team to make preparations and, ultimately, carry out the rescue. The unfolding drama generates excitement and creativity, opportunities for cross-curricular learning (e.g. science – human body) and, crucially, lots of opportunities for purposeful writing.

Clear thinking to clear writing

We have discovered that the rewards of using collaborative talk, in a variety of forms, are many and varied. When you begin to engage children in meaningful collaboration on matters that are relevant to their own lives or capture their interest, it is an experience you want to repeat as a teacher. It creates a genuine buzz among the children as they discover their thoughts and feelings in a way that they may never have done otherwise. This is exciting. It is exciting to see children developing their ideas together and being empowered because what they have to say is valued, and it is also exciting to see the impact it can have on their writing.

We all work hard to get children to be enthusiastic about what they write in school but, in my experience, this enthusiasm comes naturally when the content is self-generated through discussion that touches aspects of their own lives. All three approaches involve teachers having the confidence to retreat into the background while children enjoy extended periods of thinking and talking together. The teacher takes on the role of a facilitator. Having set the right context for shared dialogue, the teacher can then focus his/her energies on helping children to develop the language and the thinking that will enhance their writing.

Children who sometimes struggle for their own ideas are particular winners here but all children can benefit from a scaffold for their thinking – a scaffold that provides them with a 'way in' to a particular issue or question. Conceptual frames like *similar/different, cause/effect* and *alternative* can help children to make sense of complex issues. Steve Williams (2010) makes the point that we don't just think *about* concepts, we think *with* them: using them to identify and gather our own ideas and experiences. He shares a discussion he had with ten-year-old children about fairness. One example explored during the discussion involved the unfairness of getting blamed for something you didn't do. Williams offered the concept of *deserving*. Was it unfair because they felt they didn't deserve the blame? This concept enabled the children to develop one criterion for fairness which then helped the group to generate and judge further examples on the basis of getting what you don't deserve (if bad) or not getting what you deserve (if good). The concept of deserving thus helped children to develop their thinking around a particular question.

Williams argues that, as teachers take on the role of facilitator in a collaborative thinking session, it is part of their role to be sensitive to opportunities for using concepts that can enhance the dialogue and deepen thinking. He uses the term 'overlaying' to describe introducing a new or familiar concept to add meaning to children's thinking. Although it is important not to jump in too quickly, it is also important not to allow children to flounder when the simple introduction of a new concept could transform the quality and depth of the dialogue.

Some concepts are so essential to thinking, it is difficult to do any thinking of any depth without them! Not only do concepts like *criteria, reason/evidence* and *important* help to give children a foothold in discussions, they also help children to build on one another's ideas. In fact, Williams argues that without knowing how to use such concepts, children will find it very difficult to 'build on the contributions of others', which is one of the oracy requirements of the National Curriculum in England.

These concepts can be tailored for use with particular year groups and can be used as teacher prompts for 'overlaying' during joint collaborations or they can be displayed as prompts for children's thinking. They are also extremely useful for teachers who are planning joint collaborations into an English sequence. Let's say you were planning a collaboration, perhaps around a shared text, and expected 'fairness' to be a theme arising from the discussion (or had intentionally designed a collaboration question around this issue). You might do this because you wanted a deep discussion on fairness to inform a writing outcome designed around the same issue. It is a very good idea to first consider the concepts the children will need in order to explore the question in depth.

I used the concept *always/sometimes/never* to delve deeper into the issue of fairness with a Year 5 class on a transition day. We were looking ahead to the kind of class we wanted to be a part of when we embarked on a new school year in Year 6. Using the concept frame helped us to discover that, as well as *deserving*, *equality* and *need* could also be used as criteria for fairness. For example, even though everyone getting the same assessment results could be viewed as equality, we established that this would do nothing to establish who needed what help in order to improve. We also agreed that everyone getting the same amount of time from the teacher would be unfair because it didn't take into account the different needs of children in the class: it was actually fair if you got more help from the teacher than others if you really needed it.

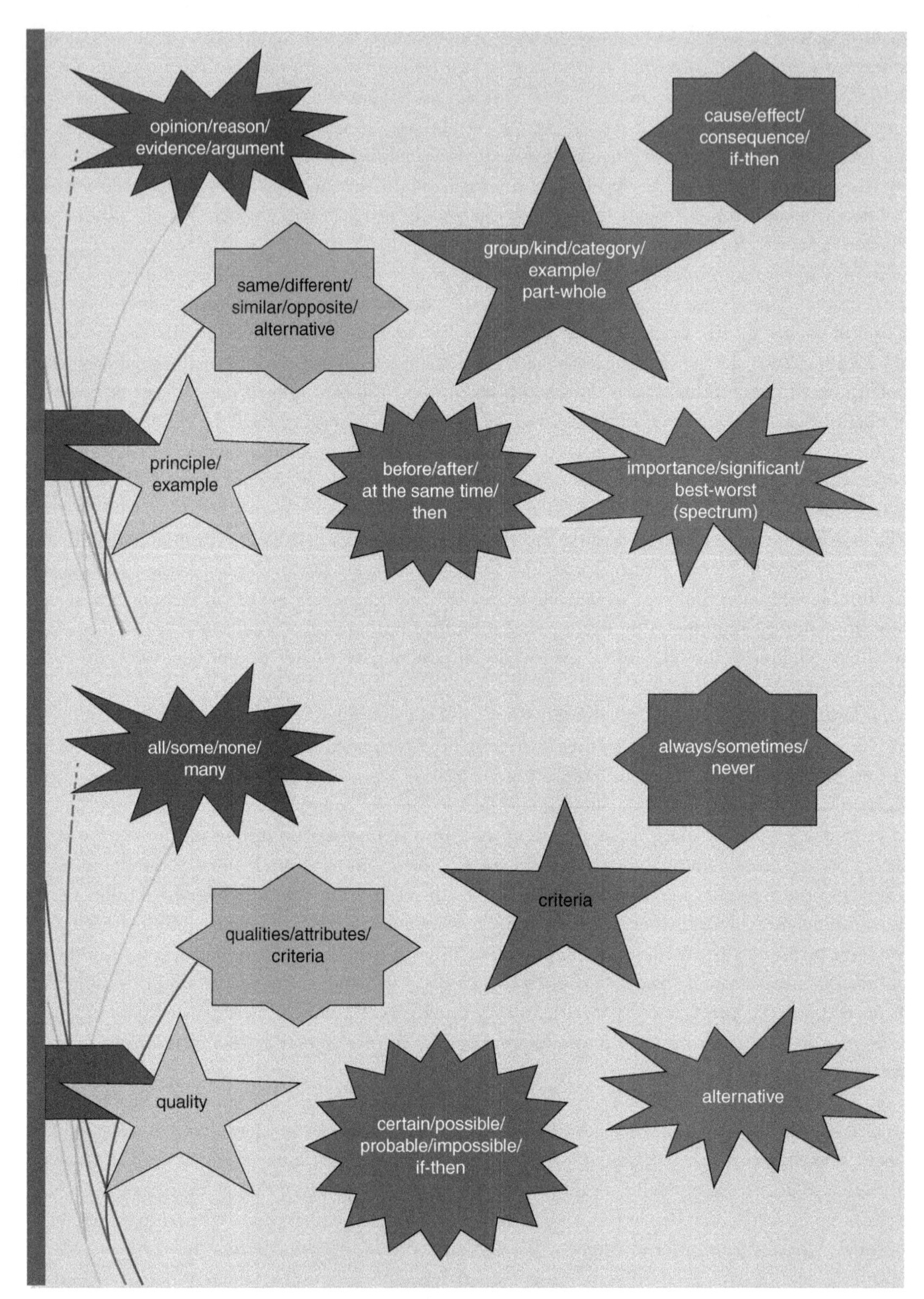

Figure 11 Some of the 'essential concepts' identified by the charity SAPARE, one of the leading providers of Philosophy for children training in the UK

Internal dialogue

Integrating collaborative thinking into the design of teaching and learning activities has another huge benefit. It improves individual thinking. In his research, Mercer (2013) noticed that the collective reasoning a child participates in with his/her peers acts as a template for the 'inner speech' of individual reasoning when the child is working alone. Dawes and Sams also found that, given the skills and opportunities for rational discussion with groups of their peers, children can develop a way of internal questioning and reflection which enables them to think through their ideas, weigh up alternatives and come to more reasoned conclusions when working individually.

'During their talk lessons and group discussions, the children were learning new combinations of words, new structures and new purposes for their talk. By doing this they seemed to assimilate a "model" for reasoning which they could use in situations where they had to puzzle something out for themselves' Dawes and Sams (2004).

Such inner speech is the basis for self-regulation. As we established when exploring feedback in Chapter 1, encouraging and guiding children to reflect on their own understanding, successes or failures, is teaching them the skills of a successful learner.

Karen Littleton and Neil Mercer are typically forthright in their evaluation of the power of collaborative thinking. 'For some children, educational success may be dependent on the extent to which school enables them to learn ways of using language as a tool for interthinking, as well as for thinking alone. This gives the quality of talk in classrooms a special significance' (Littleton and Mercer, 2013).

Reflection points

- Can we expect deep learning without children thinking more deeply?
- Is there a more natural home for thinking than collaborative talk?
- If children are to write from the heart, do they need to be given opportunities to discover their thoughts and feelings about things that matter to them?
- How can we teach children to 'think together' through carefully structured collaborations?
- Can the use of clear rules to ensure children know exactly what is expected of them make collaborative talk more productive?
- Can regular participation in Exploratory talk develop children's reasoning skills and increase attainment?
- Can the oracy requirements of the National Curriculum England be met through Exploratory talk, Philosophy for children and drama?
- Do these means of collaborative thinking help children to explore the deeper themes and meanings behind quality shared texts?
- Can these means of collaborative thinking motivate and inform children for writing?
- Can regular participation in collaborative thinking create a template for the self-talk that children need to reason and reflect when working alone?

4 Engagement

A teenage Brian Cox got a D in his mathematics A level: a result he was unhappy with. The reasons? Fledgling musical commitments and a lack of interest. It was the early 1980s and he was being swept up by the electronic sounds of a New Romantic wave of bands like Duran Duran and The Human League. He became keyboard player with local Oldham band, Dare, and then achieved something like stardom with D:Ream ('Things Can Only Get Better') in the early '90s. It was only a distraction. He would soon return to his first love – science. A love that had taken hold of him at a very early age. As a young child, he was fascinated by space travel. By the time he was six, he was collecting astronomy cards in an album. For Christmas he wanted a telescope and he dreamt of flying to Mars. He enjoyed his primary school lessons at Chadderton Hall but he was itching to go to senior school so that he could study physics instead of generic science. He was already hooked on Carl Sagan's landmark show *Cosmos*, regarded as one of the greatest TV shows ever made about science, as well as Patrick Moore's *The Sky at Night.* Patrick Moore was his childhood hero.

Professor Brian Cox is probably the best-known physicist in the world today and certainly the best-loved scientist in Britain. As presenter of the hit television series *Wonders of the Solar System* and *Wonders of the Universe*, his affable charm and infectious enthusiasm has brought science to a whole new audience. He has a knack for simplifying the most complex ideas. In short, Brian Cox makes science fun. What has been called the 'Brian Cox effect' has increased the number of people taking A Level physics by 20 per cent and the number of applications to university physics courses by over 50 per cent. To him, learning is fun – a passion – and he is still driven by the exhilaration of understanding new things. Now he is passing his love of science onto millions of TV viewers everywhere.

Asked why he eventually chose science over pop stardom, he said, 'Physics excited me more. I felt so energised by the process of learning – the intensity of learning – you don't get that very often. I like going on learning curves and doing TV has given me that but nothing's been as thrilling as the intensity of learning physics'. He has also said, 'You have to find something you're fascinated by and love doing. Most people, I think, are able to do great things if they find something that they love'.

Children learn best when they're having fun, or so goes the popular belief, but is it actually true or is Brian Cox an exception to the rule? Some say that education is the serious business of transmitting knowledge and that any time you spend having fun is taking time away from 'proper learning'. Proper learning shouldn't be fun! This is an issue that we need to be clear about because it has far-reaching implications for the way we design and deliver our teaching sequences in primary schools. In particular, the opportunities we give children to learn from quality authors, what we do to hook children in to a sequence of learning and the tasks we set for children can all be shaped by a school's take on this issue.

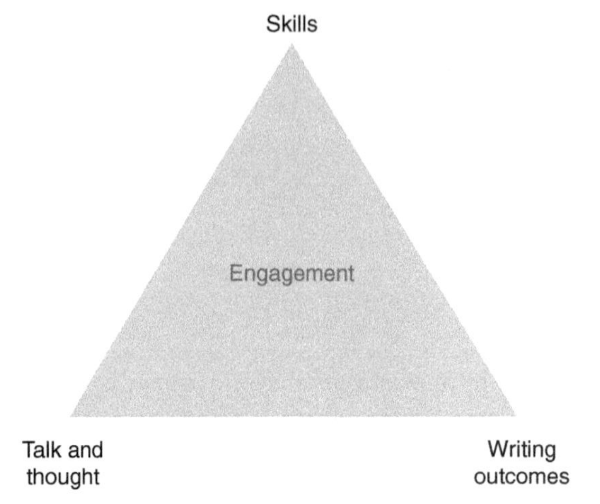

Figure 12 Engagement at the heart of the planning pyramid for English

Those who would have us believe that fun has no place in the classroom tend to argue that learning is more important than fun (in the context of the classroom). Indeed, putting the focus on fun can distract from learning. Whilst not arguing against these valid points, we must not ignore the unquestionable experience many teachers have had of lessons in which children are inspired and excited by learning experiences and learnt more as a result.

In Chapter 3, we considered how using a simple planning pyramid can guide our thoughts when conceiving of a sequence of learning in English. After thinking about where the majority of pupils are in the skills journey of their particular year group, and deciding on the next logical phase in that journey, we need then to turn our attention to the learning context. We discovered how creating opportunities for deep, collaborative thinking can have a powerful impact on children's writing. This talk is an important part of the process of engaging children in their learning.

In this chapter, we will explore how else we might harness children's enjoyment of the learning process in order to bring about maximum progress. We need to choose children's learning content and writing contexts wisely. There is a danger that writing projects in school can be somewhat abstract and subject centred. They can be removed from the lives of the children themselves and ignore what they bring to the table: their feelings, experiences, views and questions. The last thing we want to do is render children indifferent to the work they are doing so that they see it as a purely academic activity aimed at giving teachers what they want. If we accept that children's writing is at its best when it is from the heart, we must put their **engagement** at the heart of our planning and teaching.

The joy of learning

There are all sorts of things that are highly effective at distracting children from their learning: a bee in the classroom, snow or strong winds, fall-outs with friends and practically anything that moves outside the classroom window, to name but a few. We hardly need to add anything else to the list but activities that children enjoy while having little to do with the intended learning, as well as silly behaviour and showing off, can have the same effect and have no place in the classroom. Neither has the teacher taking on the role of the class clown. It is not our role to be entertainers, especially if this casts children into passive roles and robs them of opportunities to get involved and develop effective learning habits. Spending our time planning and delivering lessons in an effort to entertain our pupils is to do them a disservice, as we risk them remembering only how much fun they had instead of the intended learning.

If unnecessary entertainment that distracts children to the extent that they forget what they are supposed to be learning is bad practice, then so are aspects of lessons and teaching that strips enjoyment away. Being bored in lessons because they are so tedious is equally distracting for children. Worse still are lessons or teachers that make children feel embarrassed or intimidated. Stress is a block to effective learning. If children feel bored in a lesson or feel embarrassed or intimidated by the interaction in the room, there is a very good chance that they will remember how the lesson made them feel rather than the learning the teacher set out to achieve.

Let's consider the relevant science here. The amygdala is the part of the brain responsible for the perception of emotions such as anger, fear and sadness. Under stressful conditions, it acts as a filter and blocks the flow of information to the areas of the brain where information is stored. 'In other words, when stress activates the brain's affective filters, the learning process grinds to a halt', says former teacher and neuroscientist Judy Willis (2007). 'When we scrub joy and comfort from the classroom, we distance students from effective information processing and long-term memory storage. Students become bored, anxious, anything but engaged, and lose the joy they once felt about school.'

Stress-free classrooms promote learning by propelling information through the amygdala's filter. Not only this but, when classroom activities are pleasurable, the brain releases dopamine, a neurotransmitter that stimulates the memory centres and promotes the release of acetylcholinem, which increases focused attention. So there is a physical link between enjoyment and learning and lots of research (e.g. Pawlak et al., 2003) suggests that superior learning takes place when classroom experiences are enjoyable and relevant to students' lives, interests, and experiences. Such learning comes not from quiet classrooms and directed lectures, but from classrooms with an atmosphere of exuberant discovery (Kohn, 2004).

The key, then, is seeking to ensure children have pleasurable associations with learning. We should try to make learning enjoyable, wherever possible – not by creating meaningless add-on activities that are detached from intended learning but by seeking to ensure the process of learning is itself enjoyable. Tim Taylor, editor of imaginative-enquiry.co.uk, puts it like this: 'For some people [work and play] are at opposite ends of the spectrum, but for those that become genuinely effective learners, play and work are dimensions of the same experience – complimentary and equally important'.

We must always strive to make our classrooms as stress-free as possible and to be creative, passionate and enthusiastic about our teaching. We should aspire to make learning enjoyable – even joyful – and switch children on to learning for life.

Implications for the classroom

Let us now consider what we can do as teachers to nurture a joy of learning that will motivate children to keep wanting more, and enhance progress.

Create a safe haven

My first teaching practice as a student teacher took me to a lovely school which happened to be part of a community with more than its fair share of social problems, particularly stemming from drug and alcohol abuse. I remember the headteacher telling me that his number one priority was to ensure pupils coming into the school knew they were loved and valued and that they were safe. He knew that, unless children felt safe and relatively free from anxiety while they were at school, they wouldn't learn.

We all have the power in our own classrooms to help children to relax and enjoy the learning environment or to raise anxiety levels. It is impossible to remove stress from classrooms completely but the way we interact with children can go a long way to creating an atmosphere conducive to learning. This can be as simple as taking an interest in individuals – using downtime like break times to ask about their big football match or how their pet dog is doing. Avoiding stressful practices like calling on pupils who have not raised their hand can also make a big difference. Imagine yourself on a training course and being picked out by the course leader when you haven't quite grasped a concept or hadn't thought it through. It feels stressful, doesn't it? Perhaps stressful enough for you to avoid future courses with that particular trainer. Of course, children don't have that choice and, sometimes, providing a little more thinking time – time to exchange thoughts with a partner perhaps – is enough to get more hands in the air.

'Classrooms can provide students with emotional comfort and pleasure as well as knowledge. When teachers use strategies to reduce stress, students gain emotional resilience and learn more efficiently at higher levels of cognition' (Willis, 2007).

Use humour

Let's eat Grandma!
Let's eat, Grandma!
You see, children. Punctuation is important. It saves lives!

We established earlier that there is no place in a classroom for teachers taking on the role of class clown – prioritising entertainment over intended learning. That doesn't mean that there is no place for humour in our classrooms. It just means we have to strike the right balance. Using humour can be really effective at reducing anxiety and getting children to feel relaxed, comfortable and ready to learn.

So how do you draw the line between being educational and being distractive? By focusing on learning first, says communications researcher Jennings Bryant. Bryant, who worked as a script consultant for the children's TV show, *Sesame Street*, conducted a 22-study research project from 1969 to 2000 to examine the effectiveness of humour within education. Warning that it can be overdone – so that students are so busy waiting for the next gag that they miss the teacher's message – he advocates the use of humour so long as it is used to enhance children's attention, improve the classroom atmosphere and lower anxieties.

'Humor builds a learning relationship through the joyful confluence of head and heart', adds Ed Dunkelblau, Director of the Institute for Emotionally Intelligent Learning in the US in an interview with Edutopia Magazine (2014). 'Moreover, it brings a sense of pleasure and appreciation and creates a positive emotional experience that the students share with each other and the teacher.'

Make it relevant

Learning does not have to be boring, nor does it have to entertaining, but it does have to mean something to the learner. Making learning relevant and interesting is key if we want to fully engage children in the learning process. Children can easily get bored and, consequently, distracted from their learning, if they can't see what relevance it has to their lives. Stress levels can also rise if a lesson is overly abstract.

Get the challenge right

Finding the right level of challenge is an important aspect of making learning pleasurable and motivating for children. Here, there is a sweet spot or ideal challenge zone to strive for. Set the bar too low and our pupils will easily get bored and lose interest; set the bar too high and anxiety levels will rise. Either way, we squander precious opportunities for learning. Clearly, we need to get to know precisely what children need through ongoing assessment and be ready to match challenge with varying levels of support. While there is no merit in creating challenge for the sake of challenge, to make progress children do need an element of struggle: they need to be working just outside their comfort zone.

As previously mentioned, this involves a logically-sequenced journey through new concepts, plenty of opportunities for children to practise towards their personal targets and precise feedback on what they are doing well and how they can improve. Finding the sweet spot, where our students are being stretched but not frustrated, is not always easy but we need to be making best use of learning time and working consistently in the challenge zone will keep children engaged and moving towards their long-term aims.

Sometimes, learning is about rolling your sleeves up and 'working hard'. This doesn't mean the process isn't enjoyable. It is our job to direct learning towards personal goals; making sure we celebrate successes when goals or targets are achieved. In this way, children can develop a hunger for the next step. They can build on their neurochemical memories of positive feelings if they have opportunities to recognise and savour their successes. In his book, *Bounce*, Matthew Syed says 'where the motivation is internalised, children tend to regard practice not as gruelling but as fun' (2011).

Nothing worthwhile comes easy. There is certainly some truth in this and adults are no different from children. Take a moment to ask yourself what your favourite experiences are. Among them, for many of us, will likely be achievements that were anything but easy to come by at the time. They involved effort in our challenge zone and resulted in personal growth or that all-important feeling of pride or achievement.

Novelty

At the base of the brain, there is something called the reticular activating system (RAS), which acts as a filter for all the information that is around us – sounds, tastes, images, and so on. There can be up to two million bits of data at any time and the brain can only process so much of it. Our RAS 'filter' only lets things through that it thinks are important. How does it know what is important? By what we focus on or pay attention to most. This is the reason positive affirmations can be effective. If we focus on the positives ('I am awesome', 'I believe in myself'), then our RAS will show us things to prove that they are true for us. The more proof we see, the stronger our belief that it is true; the stronger our belief, the more likely we are to tell it to ourselves. So we need to help our pupils to set their RAS to look for the positives.

The RAS also responds to novelty. We notice anything and pay more attention to things that are new and different. This has implications for the way we teach, particularly in the way that we recap on prior learning. Once children have been taught how to punctuate direct speech, for example, they need to come back to this learning again and again to consolidate their understanding. If we can do this in different ways, rather than repeating activities in the same format, we can hold children's attention far more effectively. Perhaps children learning about speech could be asked to role play a conversation over lunch between Batman and Homer Simpson and talk about the punctuation needed. On another occasion, they could use actions for each punctuation mark when reading speech sentences out loud, or analyse examples of direct speech displayed around the class and identify any punctuation errors with a partner. Again, if children enjoy a learning activity then we are also reducing stress and increasing the likelihood of children remembering what they have learnt.

Novelty comes from variety and this also involves catering for different learning styles. Getting children up out of their seats and moving around at times – inside and outside – is important for comfort as much as catering for the kinaesthetic learner in each of us. Nobody – let alone children – enjoys sitting at a desk for hours on end. Visual prompts, including film clips and other technologies, are increasingly important to engaging today's children. For most children, the bulk of their story consumption is via digital media and can be hugely important to enhancing children's enjoyment of printed literacy, as well as a stimulus in its own right. The stunning landscapes that can be explored via game technology, for example, can provide the perfect backdrop for children's stories. Multi-sensory teaching, including lots of visual prompts and oral rehearsals, is particularly important for dyslexic children who can hold less information in short term memory and have reduced processing speed.

Independent discovery learning

In a similar way, thanks to dopamine release, children are more likely to remember and understand what they have learnt if they find it compelling or have an active role to play in figuring it out for themselves. One way of facilitating the latter is through coaching. Children work in mixed ability pairs in response to a given question: one child in the role of coach and the other in the role of coachee. Coachees say what they are thinking out loud. Coaches listen carefully and, ideally, say nothing, but if they hear their partner's thinking going off track, they prompt, question and simplify to support their efforts to figure it out for themselves, in much the same way as teachers do all day long. Coaches are not allowed to tell the answer. Children are much more likely to remember something if they have worked it out for themselves.

The coaches benefit too because their understanding is strengthened through finding the right questions to ask and finding ways to simplify concepts so that they are easier for others to understand. For thousands of years we have known that the finest way to learn something is to explain it to someone else. Children need time and practice to get used to this strategy but the more the children work in these roles (and when you have established pairs of children who work well together), the more powerful it becomes.

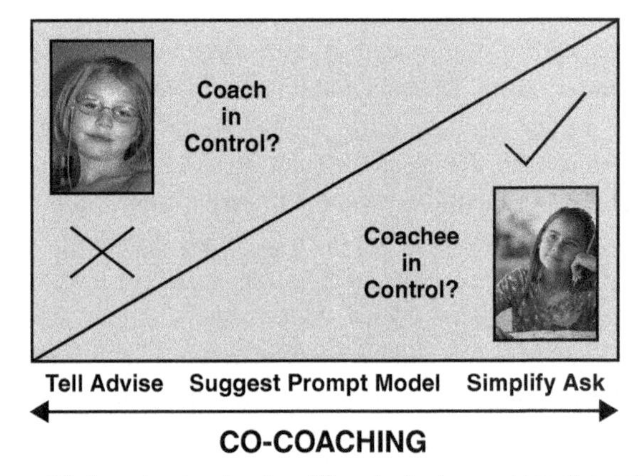

Figure 13 A poster showing the different roles in coaching discussions

In addition, Willis' research tells us that when children have some choices in the way they study or present their work, their motivation will increase and stress will diminish. They will be more accepting of their errors, motivated to try again, and less self-conscious about asking questions.

Implications for teaching writing

Planning for enjoyment in English involves careful thought about the stimuli for a sequence of lessons, including which texts to use. Getting the text choice right not only enables us to showcase the skills of a successful author but also gives us the engaging context for children's learning that we are looking for. This context can also come from other sources, such as topics in other subjects, children's experiences, imagination, interests, as well as current affairs, local legends, and so on. There are no right and wrong ways to provide this context, only relevant and irrelevant. The more we can make learning come from a place that children can identify with or that interests them, the more chance we have of getting them to write from the heart. As I have argued previously, another key ingredient is collaborative talk, which enables children to discover their thoughts, feelings and views on given subjects, and actively involves them in generating content for their writing.

Choosing an appropriate text

There are lots of reasons why it is important to get the choice of texts right when planning English sequences. Not least, they help teachers deliver on the aims of the National Curriculum, including developing good reading habits, acquiring a wide vocabulary and an understanding of grammar and language conventions, and appreciating our literary heritage. We also need the texts we choose to make children think. We need them to feed the imagination and prompt ideas that can be explored together through talk in preparation for writing. So, where to begin in making these choices?

Firstly, we need to consider the time we have and how we intend to strike a balance between different text types, including narrative fiction, poetry and non-fiction. This balance is more difficult to strike in Key Stage 2 where longer novels are among the texts we might choose. Gone are the days – and rightly so – when we used extracts from novels as the vehicle for children's learning. This robbed children of the pleasure of reading a whole story. I would suggest limiting novels to three per year in Key Stage 2: one per term. It is even worth considering not choosing a novel for the shorter spring term: the reason being that reading novels together requires a considerable amount of time.

Some schools will do this reading in the English lessons themselves and commit the whole half term – or term – to working through that text. The trouble with this approach is that it puts lots of pressure on that initial choice of text: get in wrong from the children's point of view and they could easily get bored. Secondly, it can become an exercise in 'getting through' the book in the time you have, leaving little scope for spending time exploring any deeper meanings and themes through discussion. An alternative approach is to move forward with reading the novel in reading lessons only. Content from the novel can then be chosen selectively to support learning in writing sessions, where it lends itself particularly well to the study of specific grammar features or to exploration of a wider issue, like fairness, trust or bullying.

In Year 5 or 6, for example, Charles Dickens' *A Christmas Carol*, or an abridged version, might be used. It might be chosen not only because it is a wonderful, timeless story, but also for the opportunities it presents to teach, for instance, different verb tenses, and for its powerful themes. The lessons Scrooge learns about money, love, family and happiness create rich lines of enquiry that can be explored through collaborative talk. Bringing the text into the sequence of English lessons specifically for these reasons will facilitate some reading and exploration of the text but also skills development and quality dialogue in preparation for writing. Also, taking the novel back out of the sequence when these objectives have been met will create more space in the curriculum for non-fiction texts related to topic areas, poetry, short stories and picture books.

Short and sweet

Clearly, picture books are fundamentally important to the development of literacy and language skills in EYFS and Key Stage 1, but they also have tremendous value in Key Stage 2, including Years 5 and 6. We must remember that the sophistication that most children can deal with as a reader far outstrips that which they can produce as a writer. For most children, a picture book is closer to where they are as a writer: both in terms of language and volume of text. Firstly, it is very useful for children to be able to step back from a book and see how an author has structured a whole story, from beginning to end, including plot and character development, setting detail, dialogue, and so on. When they are asked to write a story, children may be challenged to develop one or other of these aspects further, but their final outcome will not be too dissimilar in structure to a picture book. Secondly, it is often much easier to find clear, uncluttered examples of the grammar features children are asked to use in their own writing in these simpler texts than it is in sophisticated novels.

Another reason why picture books have a real place in the Key Stage 2 curriculum is that many of them offer such powerful messages in such an accessible way. Children really enjoy getting under the skin of stories to explore themes that speak to them about aspects of their own lives. Such themes are perfect starting points for Exploratory talk and creating the buzz that comes from children actively discovering that they have something to say and wanting to say it through writing.

Ideas in practice

Name: Rachael Szaloky
Teaching level: Year 5
School: Sacred Heart Primary

My Year 5 class have really loved reading the picture book, *The Invisible Kingdom* by Rob Ryan. The story is about a young prince who leads an isolated life in a huge palace. He longs to be free and explore the outside world and, one day, he discovers a trap door in his bedroom that leads to a huge attic and outside to the city of London. The boy doesn't want to be king, especially after his adventures at night time in the city.

After reading the first part of the story, I posed the 'Big Question' – 'Do you have a Plan A?'. I wanted the children to think about what they might want to become when they are older. We investigated this through discussion and explored the idea of needing to work hard now in order to achieve your goals in the future. We also used the text to explore the idea of a young boy whose destiny is already planned for him. We had lots of discussions about how this might feel and whether being 'rich' and 'royal' is actually that appealing. The story was perfect for my class to explore these themes. It was really interesting for the children to think about them in the context of a boy who lived a completely different life to theirs but, in some ways, was just the same as them. He wanted to follow his own dreams.

The text was also a great way for me to introduce my class to modal verbs and adverbs of possibility. I planned a sequence of lessons whereby children would first of all secure their knowledge of these grammar features and their understanding of their purpose. The children enjoyed spotting these within our text and then practised the skills by planning, drafting and editing their own 'speech'. The speech was written in first person as the character of the prince. They had to imagine that they were the prince, telling the nation what they wanted to do and that they should be allowed to do what they wanted to do, just like everyone else.

Spending time discussing the themes from the story really helped the children empathise with the character and get ready to write. I was really pleased with the results. They applied their new learning and used many modals and adverbs of possibility in speeches that were full of strong feelings, and showed that they had really got into the character's shoes.

Things to think about

- Have you ever found it difficult to exemplify and teach primary writing skills through a novel because of the sophistication of the text?
- Can you think of a picture book that might speak to upper Key Stage 2 children at their level and provide a stimulus for rich dialogue into writing?

For me, short stories are another must for any Key Stage 2 teacher's text list. Again, they have the advantage of offering children accessible insights into how to structure and organise stories effectively. For example, just like a primary school pupil, authors of short stories don't have much time to introduce and develop a main character, so any techniques they use are really useful for imitation in the classroom. A short story has the added benefit of featuring the same sort of aspirational language that can be found in a novel, and can also be rich in underlying themes.

When selecting a specific text to use in class, we also need a sharp focus on skills. Because of the need to put children's acquisition of grammar skills into a logical progression, I have argued that we should begin by using assessment to decide where the majority of children are up to in this skills journey. Using the appropriate Steps in Learning document (outlined in Chapter 2) as a long-term planning tool, we can pinpoint which skills they are ready for before looking for a text that helps us to teach them in context. Planning in this way means that the order in which we share texts with children is decided by our pupils' developing ability as writers, not for other reasons like having used a text at a particular time of year in the past. Allowing children to accumulate skills in a logical progression, so that they can more easily use what they already know to make sense of a new concept, can only benefit their learning.

Topic as the context

Topics led by subjects including history, geography and science provide perfect opportunities for further exploration in English. Content from topics such as space, the Fire of London, rainforests and the Titanic tends to really capture children's interest and imagination. We can make the most of this by importing topic work into English sequences to provide stimulating contexts for discussion and skills development through writing. Local authority schools library services are a wonderful source of reading materials (and artefacts) to support topic work and it is important that children are exposed to good quality non-fiction books and online reading materials, as well as fiction. Fiction books can be great sources of non-fiction writing (letters, diary entries, etc.) but only by mixing fiction with non-fiction literature can we offer our pupils a full spectrum of writing opportunities.

Teachers I have worked with have also managed to get children thinking and writing in these contexts in ways that are relevant to their lives. Examples are comparing old toys with their own after being given time to play with both; charting the journey of a chicken nugget from deforestation in the Amazon basin to make way for soya plantations to a fast food restaurant; inviting great grandparents into school to talk about their war-time experiences.

Children's experiences

A recount about a school trip is a common writing outcome in primary schools – and it's a valuable one. All the children experienced the trip and will have something to say about it, especially if it was enjoyable or something particularly exciting happened. The stand-out details will be slightly different for each child, too. One child might want to talk about how he imagined the castle's inhabitants going about their business when it was in its prime; another might want to talk about a shared joke on the bus ride home.

How often, though, do we give children an opportunity to write about other things that happen at school? In his book, *Did I Hear You Write?*, Michael Rosen shares a conversation he had with his son whose classmate Leroy had been sent home from school for punching Keith, who was racially offensive towards him. Rosen argues that here was a missed educational opportunity: racism, personal relationships, systems of punishment, and even immigration, slavery, the use and register of language could all have been made wonderfully relevant to the children's lives through talk and writing, but weren't.

Rosen argues that, although quickly brushed aside by the school, this incident would be thought about and talked about by all concerned, or not concerned but interested. Lessons would be learnt by Leroy, Keith and the teacher. What lessons? Moments like these, says Rosen, are priceless learning opportunities. It is not learning from books but from real life and we should seize upon them, discuss them and write about them because they are what matter to children.

This incident may be a little extreme but schools are hugely eventful places and there are plenty of other happenings that prompt lots of thoughts, strong feelings and talk – and, as a result, learning opportunities. Things might go missing in a class, something might be damaged, a dog might come into the school grounds, four teachers might be off sick at the same time. What's wrong with them? What happens if more teachers go off sick? Would the school close? What would you do if the school closed?

Rosen suggests that, if we want children to write thoughtful, authentic, personal writing, then they will want to be sure that we are genuinely interested in who they are. This brings children's own experiences into the mix of things we can use to inspire writing. Many of these experiences, though personal, will be common to most children. In trouble, wishes and hopes, rules and punishments, stories told by grandparents, attitudes to siblings or other members of the family, favourite dishes and recipes, work done by me (like washing the dishes), superstitions, heroes, irritating things, being fed up, my room, neighbours, and my moods are just a small number of possible starting points. Rosen says writing about such things can be another act of discovery, giving children an opportunity to reflect on experiences and remember things that were hidden or not previously thought about. They are putting a little of themselves down on the page; they have power and control to select and manipulate experiences, thoughts and ideas. 'Writing also offers the possibility of being a "real" activity and not a rehearsed one. This involves being authentic to one's own experience and ideas' (Rosen, 1998).

Music into writing

Music touches all children and it is not difficult to find artists or genres that your class is interested in or see as relevant. Songs capture all sorts of different moods. They can be fun ('The Fresh Prince of Bel-Air'), passionate (Michael Jackson's 'Earth Song'), uplifting (Journey's 'Don't Stop Believin') and can't fail to inspire children to write through their subject matter, themes, rhythm or language use. Children can learn such a lot about using language for effect from talented songwriters and poets.

We don't need to be musically inclined as teachers either. Essentially, what we are talking about is using music to inspire poetry – and of course we can use poetry to do the same thing. Asking children to write songs or poems to a set rhythm or structure and putting the results to music (or simply performing them orally) can be very powerful but, if we want children to write for truth and authenticity, then perhaps it is best if we leave the form to them. Free verse is an excellent vehicle for children to simply say what they want to say through writing. Working to a set rhyme or rhythm can often have the effect of children focusing on these elements of style rather than what they have to say. It can also be incredibly liberating and exciting for children to perform their original creations to an audience – not least because children can write without worrying too much about the correctness of sentence structure or maintaining a rhyming pattern.

That said, there are lots of skills children can practise through writing songs or poetry. From the Year 4 Steps in Learning, for example, there is no reason why composition objectives such as varied vocabulary and grammar, stylistic features (e.g. metaphors), techniques to engage the reader or audience (e.g. rhetorical questions) or organising paragraphs or verses around a theme cannot be covered in this way. Similarly, knowledge of grammar objectives such as nouns (including collective nouns), pronouns, a range of punctuation or adverbials can be used and applied just as well through some form of verse as it can through prose.

Reflection points

- Can we enhance children's progress by making the learning process more enjoyable?
- Can we give children pleasurable associations with learning by taking measures to make children feel relaxed and stress-free? By using humour appropriately? By making the learning relevant to children's lives? By getting the level of challenge right? By building novelty into teaching sequences and providing opportunities for children to discover things for themselves?
- How can our choice of texts impact on the context for skills development and collaborative thinking?
- Where can this learning context come from? Could the list include topics studied elsewhere in the curriculum, children's experiences, drama, music and poetry?

5 Practice

A four-year-old boy once begged his father to teach him to play the piano just like his sister, Maria Anna. His father was a music tutor and the boy was jealous of the attention and affection he lavished on his sister and other children who came into the house. He could see how their playing made his father happy, and longed to impress him in the same way. Despite never having considered the idea of teaching someone so young, the father – Leopold Mozart – eventually relented and began to teach his four-year-old son, Wolfgang, to play the piano. Almost immediately, he noticed that there was something different about Wolfgang. He seemed to get lost in the music. He loved to listen and he loved to play. He had an extraordinary passion for music and was so focused and determined to learn and improve – even at that incredibly young age.

With just two years' musical experience, the boy who was to become, arguably, the greatest musician who ever lived was composing his own music and wowing audiences alongside his sister in performances across western Europe: forgiving audiences who attended concerts largely for the novelty of seeing such young children play.

Mozart has often been used as an example to 'prove' the argument that talent is something you are born with, but was his talent innate or learned? A closer examination of his story is quite revealing. A number of factors – the home environment, the motivation to become a better pianist than his sister, his father's method of letting him work out his temper tantrums on challenging pieces, and the hours of performing in front of forgiving audiences – combined to make the perfect conditions to produce a musical genius. None of these factors had anything to do with innate talent.

Psychologist John Hayes spent years analysing the music and achievements of the best composers of all time. He found that all of them, including Mozart, did not produce what is considered a 'masterwork' until about ten years after they first took up music. His work confirms the findings of Anders Ericsson who suggested that it takes around 10,000 hours of deliberate practice – or about ten years' worth – to achieve expert performance in any field. So even Mozart, who was extremely lucky and had every advantage you could wish for when it comes to becoming an amazing musician, had to put in ten years of work to hone his skills to become a master.

Is it possible to reach the level of expert performance without the life advantages that Mozart enjoyed? Yes, it is. Distance runner Mo Farah was born into poverty in war-torn Somalia, in 1983. He shared a basic shack with seven other people before moving to London at the age of eight. The move meant he was separated from his twin brother, Hassan, and he did not speak a word of English. It was his PE teacher at Isleworth and Syon School that first recognised his ability and encouraged him to take up athletics. Mo is arguably the best runner Britain has ever produced and is certainly the most decorated. He said that his humble beginnings taught him that you have to work for what you get in life. He also said, 'The most important thing is commitment. I don't dream of winning – I train for it'.

Words like these from Mo Farah offer a perfect antidote to what I call an X-Factor mentality among some primary-aged children: the idea that your talent will one day be discovered and success will follow – without a great deal of effort on your part. For me, the idea that almost anybody can reach expert level if they work hard enough is a tremendously inspiring concept to take into the classroom. It shows that having high expectations of all children is an absolute must, and so is believing in them and helping them to believe in themselves.

Lessons from Mozart and Mo

What can we take away from Mozart and Mo Farah's stories that is useful with regard to developing writing skills in the classroom? Clearly, practising is key to writing success but it is not just any old practise that makes perfect.

Anders Ericsson says 'the right sort of practice carried out over a sustained period of time leads to improvement. Nothing else'. So, what is 'the right sort of practice'? In his book, *Peak – How All of Us Can Achieve Extraordinary Things,* Ericsson does a great job of exploding some popular myths:

- Our abilities are limited by our genetics
- If you do something for long enough, you're bound to get better at it
- Effort is all you need to improve: if you just try hard enough, you'll improve. If you want to get better at full stops, try harder. If you want to improve your spelling, try harder.

Ericsson's 'deliberate practice' mindset offers a very different view: anyone can improve but it requires the right approach, not just more time and effort. If you're not improving, it's not because you lack innate talent, it's because you're not practising in the right way. Deliberate practice involves getting outside your comfort zone in a focused way, with clear goals and a way to monitor your progress.

Mozart did not just spend hour after hour pounding out the same tunes on a piano. He constantly pushed his limits by taking on new, challenging compositions and his father was on hand to monitor his progress and offer precise feedback. Effort is all you need to improve? Tell that to Mo Farah who had already committed up to eight hours a day to training for ten years before he uprooted his family from their London home to work with his new coach, Alberto Salazar, in Portland, Oregon, in 2011. At this point, Farah still had his biggest achievements on the track ahead of him and he has since admitted that, before he went to work with Salazar, his technique was 'all over the place'. It is likely that he would never have achieved the incredible success he did if he had not changed the way he practised.

We don't have 10,000 hours or ten years to work with our primary school pupils on their writing skills but then the aim is not to make them writing experts. What we do have is at least seven academic years in which a substantial amount of time is devoted to writing on a daily basis. By anyone's standards, this represents a fantastic opportunity for mastery learning: to help children along the road to independent and fluent application of a wide range of writing skills for different purposes. Our task as teachers is to ensure that, when children spend time practising their writing skills in school, they are practising in the right way.

Deliberate practice in the classroom

Here are the ways we can apply the principles of deliberate practice in our schools.

1. Determine what each child needs to work on

Rather than working on what they are already good at, deliberate practice requires that you work on those things that you *are not good at* – yet. So children need their teacher's help to identify the next step (or set targets) towards their long-term aim.

2. **Give each child feedback on their targets**

   Feedback is one of the most important aspects of deliberate practice. Children need to be constantly aware of what they are doing well and where they can improve. Involving the children in setting and reviewing progress against targets and being precise with feedback can help children to self-reflect and become less dependent on teacher feedback over time.

3. **Children work on the aspect they need to improve**

   Each child practises the skills that have been recognised as the next steps in their development. If a tennis player continuously hit forehand shots long, he/she would have to adjust – perhaps putting more top-spin onto the ball. If a child consistently wrote proper nouns without capital letters, he/she would need to re-focus on the rules – perhaps using an action for names of people and places to remind him/her to include a capital when reading the sentences back. Based on your feedback, and their own reflection, they improve their skills.

4. **Repeat**

   Repetition is absolutely crucial for the development of children's skills. Going through this deliberate practice process one time will not do anything. Children need to be given plenty of opportunities across different subjects to hone their skills for as long as it takes until the skill is part of their writing toolkit.

From unconscious incompetence

To help children to achieve their long-term aim, each teacher has to guide them through the different stages involved in acquiring new skills.

It is helpful, here, to consider the work of Noel Burch who developed the Conscious Competence Model of learning in the 1970s. The model is useful for teachers, if only for the reassurance of knowing that there are clear stages to the process of learning and one of them is when learners can't do things they are trying to do! It can help teachers to stay in touch with how their pupils are feeling as they gain competence so that they are ready to give plenty of encouragement. It is particularly useful, in the context of this book, however, to know that the final stage involves having such control over what we are doing that we can do it very well without even being aware of the skills we are using.

Children beginning a new year group start off at the 'unconscious incompetence stage': they don't know what they don't know or can't do. Most lack the knowledge and skills to write at the level they should be able to write at by the end of the year.

Conscious incompetence

When the teacher introduces a new writing skill, children become aware of what they cannot do. They become 'consciously incompetent'.

We have already addressed the need – particularly for younger children – for work on new skills to be carried out in a very positive environment in which they are shown what success looks like. Mistakes are welcomed and used to promote learning and lots of advice, encouragement and feedback is offered to guide children through their early efforts. That's because this stage can be demoralising, causing people to lose confidence or even give up on their learning efforts altogether. Use of positive affirmations can be useful here: simple things like 'I am awesome!' and 'I believe in myself and my abilities' can help them to focus on work more positively and instill confidence and self-belief.

Hopefully, it won't be too long before we teachers can celebrate small successes with less confident learners and prove that their self-belief and effort does pay off. It can be very powerful for children who are experiencing a moment of self-doubt to show them what their focused effort has enabled them to achieve in the past: 'Remember when all your words used to be squashed together? And just look at the lovely spaces between your words now. We can do anything if we practise'.

Conscious competence

Practice – or more specifically deliberate practice involving focused effort on next steps, feedback and repetition – is key to moving to the 'conscious competence' stage. Here, children know they have acquired the skills and knowledge they need. They put their learning into practice regularly and gain confidence as they use their new skills. Children still need to concentrate on their new skills to maintain conscious control over them and it is our job as teachers to provide them with varied opportunities across the curriculum to use them often. The more practice and experience children get, the more automatic their application becomes. They enter the 'unconsciously competent' stage.

Unconscious competence

This is the stage we are aspiring to get children to reach as teachers of writing: the stage in which children are using their new skills effortlessly because they have mastery over them. They are able to apply their new learning into different contexts without conscious effort because they have committed the learning to long-term memory and can leave the performance to their unconscious minds. Have you ever had the realisation, while driving, that you have covered a considerable distance and yet don't remember anything about that part of the journey: what you did or what was going on around you on the roads? That is because you have developed a degree of mastery over the skills involved in driving. You can get where you want to go, keeping yourself and other road users safe, without consciously thinking about the individual tasks you need to perform. It just seems easy.

Similarly, children can use their writing skills without thinking about them too much and are confident of success. At this stage, once children have mastered one set of skills, they are open to new challenges and are ready to begin the process again to acquire new skills.

The model highlights the constant need to consolidate previously learnt skills as well as tackling new ones, and particularly the central role to be played by deliberate practice. We teachers need to ensure we set aside plenty of time in the curriculum for children to work on their personal targets – the challenges that we have decided will enable them to take their next steps in their journeys as writers. In Chapter 2, we focused on *what* children need to learn. It is crucial that each teacher is absolutely clear on what the step-by-step acquisition of skills looks like in their year group. Let's now turn our attention to what deliberate practise might involve in relation to *how* children might best acquire the skills that underpin confident, accurate and fluent writing.

We will take a brief look at practising phonics and spelling (key building blocks for confident writing) before focusing on teaching grammar in context, with particular reference to the techniques of shared and guided writing: important ways of focusing children's thinking and developing confidence in their own practice. We will then consider implications for differentiation – the need for support and challenge for different children – as they practise in English and across the curriculum.

Practising phonics

Many believe that it is actually during writing, rather than reading, that phonic knowledge comes to the forefront and really develops (Winsor and Pearson 1992). In attempting to write new words, children have to listen for the sounds in those words and write letters or letter strings to represent those sounds, often repeating the sounds out loud as they do so. It is important for teachers to provide children with many and varied opportunities for reading and writing while they are developing their phonic knowledge. These opportunities should extend way beyond the printed resources used for systematic phonics instruction.

In their book, *Teaching Phonics in Context*, David Hornsby and Lorraine Wilson (2011) argue that the teaching and learning of phonics should be a part of 'genuine literacy events' and that children should spend much more time reading and writing (thereby learning to apply their phonic knowledge) than they do in the actual study of sound-letter relationships.

If children get opportunities to apply their phonics skills to functional and interesting reading and writing activities, they practise associating meaning with new words and can develop mastery in using them. Similarly, as they progress through the stages of spelling development, children need to be encouraged to attach meaning to words, making use of a range of spelling strategies as they do so. Emmitt et al. (2013) say that, if children continue to spell mainly by sound, they will remain immature spellers because they have insufficient resources to draw upon.

Practising spelling

The teaching of spelling should build on the teaching of phonics in EYFS and Key Stage 1, and should be equally systematic, but how do we help children to attach meaning to new words, and what are the spelling strategies we can help them to employ?

Attaching meaning to new words is about using them in context. It is more difficult to plan writing opportunities around new spelling rules, prefixes or suffixes in Key Stage 2. This is because there are more vocabulary, grammar and punctuation skills for teachers to think about and, as I argued in Chapter 2, it is these skills that should drive teachers' thinking when they are planning sequences of learning in English. I'm a big believer in keeping the planning process as simple as possible and trying to accommodate spelling as well as grammar objectives when you are planning contextual writing opportunities can get confusing. However, if we plan for the application of grammar skills in the first instance, we can then consider which spelling skill the planned writing outcome lends itself to.

In practice

For example, a useful writing outcome for Year 5 children might be a letter of application (perhaps to become a member of the school council) in which they are encouraged to promote their skills and personal qualities. The main driver may be to give children an excellent opportunity to use modal verbs (e.g. *would, could*) and adverbs of possibility (e.g. *perhaps, certainly*). Such a writing task would be equally useful for children to practise the -ible, -able, -ibly, -ably suffixes. A brief brainstorm amongst children would generate lots of application ideas – such as *responsible*, *reliable*, *incredibly* and *considerable* – and allow for recap of the spelling rules before writing. If the opportunity for children to apply a newly-learnt spelling skill is not there, then our attention should turn to consolidating a skill learnt previously (even if it was originally taught in a previous year group).

If we want children to commit learning to long-term memory, we need to get them to think for themselves. Challenging children to expand their vocabulary and apply their new-found knowledge of words requires deeper thought about the meaning of words and whether they are appropriate in particular contexts. Dialogue around different vocabulary choices, including newly-learnt spellings, can find a natural home in guided reading, where the meanings of unfamiliar words are discussed in context, and shared writing, where the effect on meaning of different word choices can be considered. Combined with a variety of spelling strategies children can turn to, these experiences can create the neural footprint to help children store and retrieve words.

Spelling strategies

To make maximum progress in spelling, children not only need to be able to use their phonological knowledge but also need to develop other knowledge and strategies to help them to spell new words. They need a visual awareness that will help them to recognise other words that look the same or have the same spelling patterns. It will often help children to write new words down to see if they look right. They need an understanding of word roots, prefixes, suffixes and spelling rules (morphological knowledge) and an understanding of word origins can also equip them for successful spelling (etymological knowledge). Spelling instructions that explore word structure, word origin and word meaning are the most effective, even though students with dyslexia may still struggle with word recall.

One of the great strengths of English is its huge vocabulary, much of which is borrowed from other languages. This does, however, present its spelling challenges. At times, the origins of words can help children's understanding. For example, the Germanic origins of the silent *k* encountered by children in Year 2 can help children understand the spelling of some of the words in their curriculum. In German, every sound is pronounced so the letter *k* in the word *knecht*, the German word for servant, is heard when the word is spoken. Around 600 years ago, there were strong Germanic influences on the English language so the distinctive clicking sound of the *k* would be heard at the beginning of words like *knee*, *knock* and *knight*. Only after the invention of the printing press, in the mid 15th century, did the letter become silent. In Year 3 and 4, children can learn that it is the Greek origin of words like *mystery*, *Egypt* and *pyramid* that gives the *i* sound its *y* spelling.

Effective teaching of spelling, then, demands that teachers are very knowledgeable about spelling and the teaching of spelling. The appropriateness of each strategy will vary. For a word like *recognise*, a child might be encouraged to draw on his/her phonic knowledge, splitting the word up into syllables (re-cog-nise) to focus on each sound in the word. For a word like *would*, a Year 2 child might be encouraged to use his/her visual awareness to recognise the letter pattern *ould*, perhaps writing the word down to see if it looks right or using the mnemonic 'oh you lucky duck' to memorise it. Remembering this pattern will help him to spell the words *could* and *should*. Children in Year 3 and 4 should use their morphological knowledge for a word like *disappointed*, splitting it up into parts: the word root *appoint*, the prefix *dis-* and the suffix *-ed*. If children can spell the word root and have an understanding of prefixes and suffixes, they are likely to spell the new word correctly.

Regular use of these strategies as part of a whole-school programme of spelling teaching will enable children to become highly resourceful spellers. This is important not only for assessment purposes but because accurate spelling is one of the foundation stones upon which confident writing is built. Each class teacher has to be clear about their part of the spelling progression and have the knowledge needed to teach children the different strategies they need to learn new spellings.

Grammar for writing

To write effectively, children have to be able create meaning, conjure mental images and stir emotional reactions from their readers. Grammar provides children with the toolkit they need. It is not sufficient for them to recognise parts of speech and have some knowledge about their function. They need to become increasingly skilled at experimenting with language, learning through the experience of writing the meaning and effects these elements of grammar can create. This takes practice and lots of it.

Sometimes teachers can be guilty of diving immediately into the grammar teaching but, if we want children to write effectively for purpose, we need to firstly focus their attention on *what* effects they can create and only then on *how* they can create them. This begins with analysing the work of skilled authors.

In practice

For example, I often use the work of Chris Priestley when teaching Year 6 children how to create a mysterious/spooky atmosphere in their narrative writing. The following extracts follow in quick succession at the beginning of the first of his *Tales of Terror from the Black Ship* called 'The Storm':

> *'... the coast had been savaged by a wild and rabid storm.'*

> *'... [my home] stood on a gnarled promontory that had been gnawed relentlessly over the centuries... It was eaten away on either side like the core of an apple...'*

Here, the author creates the mental image of a home just about hanging onto existence because of the power of storms and the sea. The building, and as a result its occupants, seems incredibly vulnerable and we as readers already feel a little anxious for our main character. This is the effect of the writing. One of the ways Chris Priestley has achieved this is his personification of the storm and the sea and another is his use of the passive voice, which emphasises the results of a given action (the savaging, the gnawing and the eating) rather than the action itself.

We want children to focus on what they are trying to achieve and to be discerning about the choices they make from an increasing range of language skills. The focus of the dialogue we have with our pupils, then, should be on meaning and impact. How a particular grammatical feature helps children to achieve what they are setting out to communicate in their writing will form part of that dialogue. Of course, this requires children to be clear on the purpose of their writing and what they want to achieve. To develop the notion of writing as design – designing something to achieve a particular aim – Debra Myhill and her colleagues suggested using a set of prompts such as these:

Writing as design

- What do I want to communicate?
- What effects do I want to achieve?
- What is the best way to say this?
- How do I want it to look?
- How do I design this for my reader?
- Does it work? Is it any good?

If we work in this way, ensuring we are not implying one correct way of writing, we can be sure that our role as teachers of grammar is not simply to pass on tricks and techniques so that they can be replicated in a mechanistic way. Rather, we are encouraging children to behave as published writers do, and helping them to gain conscious control over more and more features of grammar in a wider range of contexts. We are opening up a wider range of possibilities to them as speakers and writers.

Choices and possibilities

Debra Myhill's research (2012) found strong evidence that the right kind of grammar teaching improves children's writing skills. More than that, it reminds us that good teaching of writing is about helping children to develop a repertoire of skills for communicating effectively through writing, through moulding language like putty.

> *'Students need to see the huge variety of ways that they can shape language for effect. Being explicit about grammar can draw their attention to how different language patterns can create different relationships with the reader' (Myhill et al., 2012).*

Myhill refers to this as the magic of words. A key message from her research is that we teachers need to be ready to help children to experiment with language far more than we have done in the past. This is to avoid the prescriptive, formulaic writing that has not been the intention of national policy in England but has certainly been the effect. Like Cecilia Busby and her author contemporaries, mentioned in Chapter 2, Myhill and her colleagues found that lots of children's work was characterised by the 'adding' principle, with many children interviewed explaining that to improve their writing they needed to add more adjectives/adverbs, and so on.

In order to raise expectations for writing, we need to be ready to shake off these extremely limiting perceptions. They have no place in classrooms where we aspire to deeper and mastery learning. In mathematics, we lead children into deeper learning by encouraging them to explore different ways of tackling a problem. We can do the same in writing – where there are even more possibilities open to us. Fear of failure is a big enemy in writing lessons: children are often inhibited from writing anything that could be perceived as being wrong. Yet all professional writers know that not all ideas work, and producing a text that suits a particular purpose involves trying things out, changing your mind and discounting some ideas altogether. The natural home for such experimentation is shared writing.

Using shared writing

Pie Corbett describes becoming a better writer as a journey where the teacher is a child's companion and guide, showing the way and offering challenge at every turn until he/she eventually finds his/her own path. In this analogy, shared writing has to be the principal mode of transport on the journey. 'It is the key moment at which writing is taught. Teachers who do not do shared writing are not teaching writing' (Corbett, 2015). Shared writing is completed with the class before children write independently. It involves demonstration, where the teacher gives a running commentary while showing how to do something new, and joint composition, where the children do more of the thinking and composing, explaining their choices as they do so.

The pace should be fairly brisk to hold attention and promote excitement as the text emerges but there should be pauses for thinking time, re-reading and discussion around alternative ideas. This quality dialogue around a shared text helps children develop their self-talk habits that see them deciding between different language choices and questioning themselves about whether a particular word or expression works and how it sounds when they re-read it.

In practice

One shared write in my Year 6 class involved introducing a new character into a story. In a previous unit, we had explored the techniques that Gene Kemp used in his short story, *Toothie and the Cat*, including expanded noun phrases. In this new unit, we considered how Frank Cottrell-Boyce employed different techniques in his book, *Millions,* to introduce the main characters, Damian and his brother Anthony. Unlike Kemp, who packs a couple of opening paragraphs with detail about Toothie and then Cat, Cottrell-Boyce uses a technique I call 'show not tell' to gradually drop hints about Damian and Anthony into the narrative through what they say, think and do – or what others say to/about them.

I wanted my pupils to learn how to use this technique as part of our work on character description so 'show not tell' was the focus of our early analysis of *Millions*, and subsequent shared write. Sometimes when I do a shared write with Year 6, I change the context slightly to increase the challenge for pupils by asking them to transfer their learning back into the context of our agreed writing outcome. This time, the shared write focused on the arrival in school of an imagined new supply teacher. The idea was to prepare children to introduce a dog-catcher character into our ongoing *Toothie and the Cat*-inspired story involving a homeless man who strikes up an unlikely friendship with a stray dog.

> *"Who's that?" said Liam.*
>
> *Before Daniel could answer, the new supply teacher strode menacingly into the Year 6 classroom. He barked a "good morning" and fixed child after child with a piercing glare that snapped the chatty children into silence. Then he turned and wrote his name in perfect capital letters on the whiteboard.*
>
> *"I am Mr Spinks," said Mr Spinks. "I am here to teach. You are here to sit silently, listen and learn."*
>
> *This is going to be a long day, thought Daniel.*

The demonstration part of this session took us up to *'good morning'*. By this time, my commentary had made my thinking explicit on the apostrophe in the opening sentence, speech punctuation and the need for a comma to mark the pause in the second sentence. I had also asked, and the children had told me, that the way somebody does or says something can reveal things about their character. In my commentary, I played with several alternatives – *said, muttered, offered* – before deciding upon the verb *barked*. Originally, the word *menacingly* wasn't in my script but one child suggested it and together we questioned whether it usefully added to the meaning of the sentence: was it even possible to stride menacingly? Another child was sure it was and promptly demonstrated and we agreed that the word further hinted at the supply teacher's character.

As the children took more control of the text, they offered ideas around the teacher's piercing look and the class being stunned into silence. With prompting, they were able to go further with the 'show not tell' description: Mr Spinks' words, Daniel's reaction and even the subtle inclusion of the perfect handwriting (which the children felt matched the teacher's strictness) all contributed to the character introduction.

Teaching in this way involves opening up discussion at every turn rather than closing it down. It allows children to witness a writer (the teacher) in action while also involving them in producing a model text. As well as highlighting a specific learning focus, it presents the opportunity to recap on relevant prior learning, especially skills that are target areas for children in the class (such as using apostrophes, direct speech and commas in the above example). Working on these skills with the teacher can give children the confidence they need to take next steps in their own writing.

Using guided writing

For some children, all the whole-class teaching in the world won't help them to move forward as writers. What they need is hands-on support as they work on their individual targets.

A teacher can't address the individual needs of all his/her pupils at the same time. He/she needs to carefully plan how to divide his/her time between different groups of pupils. As previously mentioned, this involves using assessment to group children, not in broad-brush ability groups but according to specific shared needs. It is tremendously powerful for children to have their teacher on hand to remind them of advice and strategies and to prompt their thinking as they try things and make mistakes.

Guided writing is deliberate practice in action. Thanks to the teacher's immediate and precise feedback, children are constantly aware of what they are doing well and where they can improve. With time to reflect on their feedback and respond independently, as the teacher turns his/her attention to other children in the class, target children can take big strides forward as writers.

Differentiation

As they practise their writing skills, then, some children need support. This does not mean working on tasks beneath the expectations of their peers, as was the case with traditional forms of differentiation. Doing this routinely risks those children falling further behind and, over time, can lower their expectations of themselves. Instead of simplifying the task, we need to find ways of simplifying the thinking around the task. This will often take the form of adult support for planning or guided writing but it might also include children planning in coaching pairs or mixed ability groups, working with visual or word prompts, engaging in simple physical activities or experiences to support writing, or using a writing frame that provides a loose structure for a text.

For other children – those who already demonstrate conscious control of a wide range of skills – we need to provide further challenge. In the past, such children have been 'accelerated' to work on more sophisticated skills – before they have had a chance to deepen their understanding of earlier concepts and skills. Teaching for shallow learning in this way can look great on skill tick lists but denies children the opportunity to really hone their skills and become the best communicators they can be. For these children, the challenge needs to come increasingly through the context. Just like young mathematicians need more complex problems to deepen their thinking, young writers need to be taken out of their comfort zone into more challenging contexts. They need tasks that deepen their thinking and build resilience and determination as they move to unconscious competence. How do we create these more challenging contexts? Teachers need a straightforward way to routinely build further challenge into their planning. We need look no further than Bloom's Taxonomy, a model to promote higher order thinking in education developed in 1956 by Dr Benjamin Bloom, and revised in 2001. Figure 14 is part of a table of questions and key words that is an excellent resource for doing just that – for reading and writing. The complete table can be found in Appendix 3.

In practice

As part of a history topic on the Titanic, my Year 6 class considered the circumstances leading to its demise with the tragic loss of 1,503 lives. The children had researched the timeline of events on April 14, 1912, before taking part in an Exploratory talk: 'What caused the sinking of the Titanic?'. Some blamed communication failings in the ship's last hours, some pointed to a fire that raged in its coal bunkers before it even set sail and others put it down to an unfortunate sequence of events.

The children were then tasked to write a newspaper article reporting the outcome of the British public inquiry. They got the opportunity to re-write history in their article, deciding what they considered the appropriate outcome and explaining how the tragedy came about. Inspiration for a challenge group task was drawn from the 'Evaluating' section of the Bloom's table, specifically the word *criticise* and the stem *Assess the importance of...* As most were of the opinion that the fire was the biggest contributory factor in the disaster, the children were challenged to use their article to criticise the White Star Line for sending the doomed liner to sea, despite knowing about the blaze.

The shift in context required deeper thinking on the part of the challenge group. Like the rest of the class, they were asked to include direct and reported speech, which had been the grammar focus of the week, and explain how the ship came to sink. However, they now had to think more carefully about the purpose of their article and the desired effect of the criticism on their readers.

ACE IT!

I like to call the above shift in context an ACE IT! challenge. While planning for skills development through meaningful writing tasks, teachers can consult the Bloom's Taxonomy prompt sheet to consider how more fluent writers can be challenged: how they can be tasked to think more deeply about applying their skills.

With regards to the IT! part of the technique, what do we mean by 'fluent' application? Children who don't read fluently devote much of their cognitive energy to decoding individual words and phrases, making it difficult for them to focus on the meaning of what they read. Similarly, children lacking writing fluency devote lots of cognitive energy to forming individual words or basic sentence structures, making it

LEVEL 4 – ANALYSING		LEVEL 5 – EVALUATING		LEVEL 6 – CREATING	
Examine and break evidence into parts by identifying motives or causes. Make inferences and find evidence to support generalisations.		Present and defend opinions by making judgements about information, validity of ideas or quality of work based on a set of criteria.		Compile information together in a different way by combining elements in a new pattern or proposing alternative solutions.	
key words	**Questions**	**key words**	**questions**	**key words**	**Questions**
Analyse categorise compare conclusion contrast discover distinguish divide examine function inference inspect list motive relationships simplify survey take part in test for theme	What are the parts of…? How is… related to…? Why do you think…? What is the theme…? What motive is there…? What conclusion can you draw…? How would you classify…? How would you categorise…? What evidence can you find…?	assess award choose compare conclude criticise decide defend evaluate explain importance judge justify opinion prioritise prove rate recommend select support	Do you agree with the actions … / outcome…? What is your opinion of…? How would you prove/ disprove…? Assess the value/ importance of… Would it be better if…? What would you recommend…? How would you defend the actions…?	adapt build change choose combine create develop elaborate happen imagine improve invent make up maximise minimise modify plan predict propose solution	What changes would you make to…? How would you improve…? What would happen if…? Can you elaborate on the reason…? Can you propose an alternative…? Can you invent…? How would you adapt… to create a different…? How could you change (modify) the plot (plan)…? What could be done to minimise/ maximise…? Suppose you could … What would you do…?

Figure 14 Key words and prompts using Bloom's taxonomy

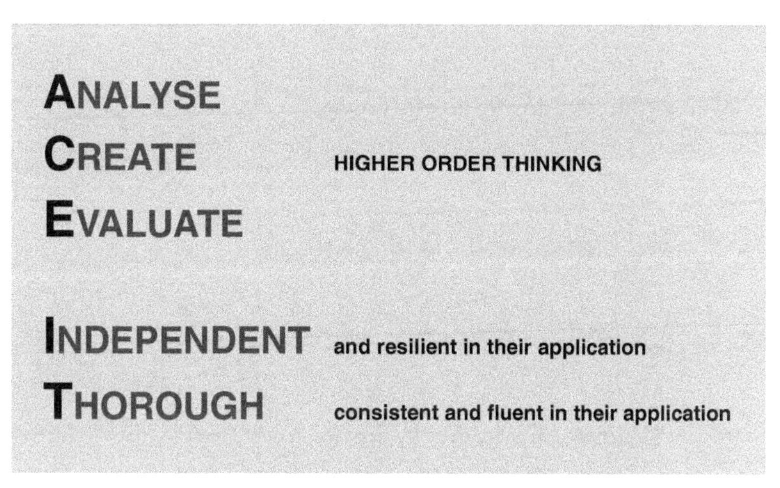

Figure 15 The ACE IT! acronym

harder for them to focus on conveying their thoughts and feelings effectively. Fluency comes from reading and from regular practice of skills, experimenting with different language choices under the teacher's guidance, and writing for meaningful purposes. Children will also need to show that they can apply skills consistently over time and demonstrate resilience when applying skills in more complex contexts.

In this way, assessment and feedback conversations become much more holistic, focusing on developing genuine mastery learning. The alternative is a shallow focus on whether boxes can be ticked for more individual skills that have, for whatever reason, been adjudged to represent 'deeper learning'.

In practice

Figure 16 shows a child's writing which has been rewarded with an 'ACEd IT!' stamp for her response to an ACE IT! challenge. The writing came from some work in Year 6 on the story of *Cinderella*. The story was chosen to take the pressure off children with regards to plot so that they could channel their creative energies into descriptive writing. A particular focus was authors' use of internal dialogue to develop a character through thoughts and feelings. The children got an opportunity to discuss how Cinderella was feeling, particularly after the visit of her fairy godmother. The hot seating technique was used to put several children into role as Cinderella to explore her character further before the class was asked to write this part of the story.

The ACE IT! challenge group was asked to tackle the writing task from a slightly different angle. The question stem *How would you adapt…* under the 'Creating' section of the Bloom's table was used to make the context of their writing more challenging. They were asked to imagine that there was no fairy godmother in the story, but Cinderella still went to the ball!

Practise across the curriculum

If you want to become a better football player, you have to play football regularly. Yes, it is worth spending time practising individual skills like tackling or taking corners, but ultimately you have to be able to apply

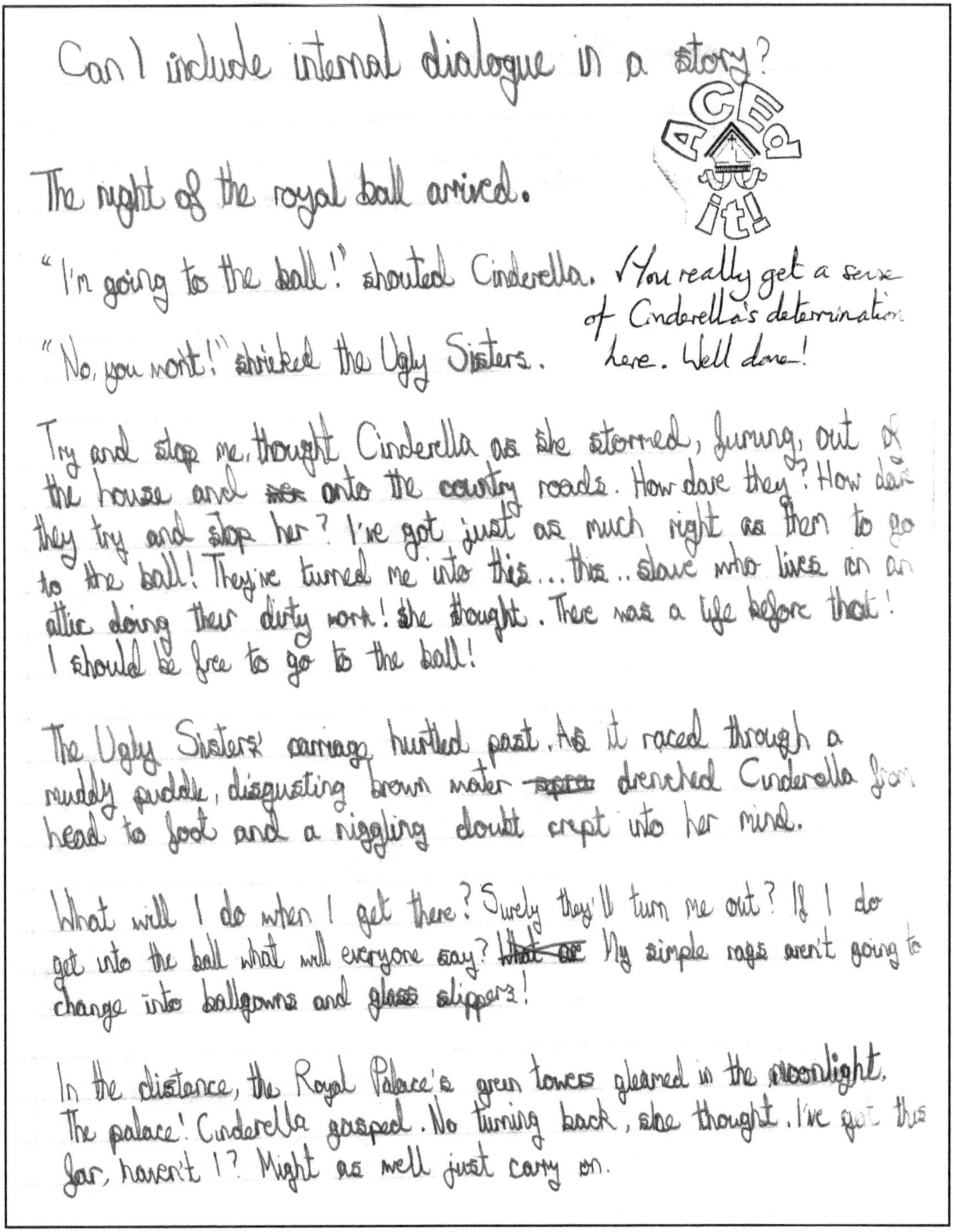

Can I include internal dialogue in a story?

ACEd it!

The night of the royal ball arrived.

"I'm going to the ball!" shouted Cinderella. ✓You really get a sense of Cinderella's determination here. Well done!

"No, you won't!" shrieked the Ugly Sisters.

Try and stop me, thought Cinderella as she stormed, fuming, out of the house and ~~ne~~ onto the country roads. How dare they? How dare they try and stop her? I've got just as much right as them to go to the ball! They've turned me into this... this.. slave who lives in an attic doing their dirty work! she thought. There was a life before that! I should be free to go to the ball!

The Ugly Sisters' carriage hurtled past. As it raced through a muddy puddle, disgusting brown water ~~spra~~ drenched Cinderella from head to foot and a niggling doubt crept into her mind.

What will I do when I get there? Surely they'll turn me out? If I do get into the ball what will everyone say? ~~What ar~~ My simple rags aren't going to change into ballgowns and glass slippers!

In the distance, the Royal Palace's green towers gleamed in the moonlight. The palace! Cinderella gasped. No turning back, she thought. I've got this far, haven't I? Might as well just carry on.

Figure 16 Child's writing rewarded with ACEd IT! stamp

these skills successfully in a game we aim to win. Similarly, if we want to get better at writing, we have to write regularly. There is a time and place for working on capital letters or adverbs, but ultimately we need to be able to apply skills in such a way that they help us to achieve a particular purpose in writing.

Schools will have their own policies with regard to the amount of time they expect to be devoted to writing. I think that we should aim to get children writing every day. There may be very good reasons why this doesn't take place in an English lesson (because the lesson is primarily devoted to oral dialogue, for example) but we should do our utmost to make space for writing somewhere in the curriculum.

Writing in subjects other than English has the inherent value of providing children with a different context in which to apply their developing writing skills (unless, of course, a topic from another subject is providing the stimulus and content for a writing outcome in English). An important part of the mastery journey is to continually provide new and challenging contexts for writing. Our expectations should be just as high as they are in English and, crucially, children should be encouraged to put in the same amount of effort to achieve their personal targets. Otherwise, we risk wasting opportunities for children to take those all-important next steps as writers.

Reflection points

- Do the experiences of the best (Mozart, Mo Farah, etc.) teach us the value of finding the right approach to practise to hone our skills?
- Does deliberate practice – involving setting individual targets for children, providing repeated opportunities for practice and giving regular feedback – provide us with the best strategy for maximising children's progress as writers?
- How can we provide plenty of meaningful reading and writing activities to help children practise their phonics and spelling skills?
- How can we help children develop a number of strategies to become resourceful spellers? Should those strategies include use of phonological knowledge for letter-sound correspondence and syllable structure; use of visual awareness to recognise spelling patterns; use of morphological knowledge to understand word roots, prefixes, suffixes and spelling rules; and use of etymological knowledge for understanding of word origins?
- Can we encourage fluent, creative and individual writing by giving children opportunities to learn from quality authors and experiment with different language choices?
- How important is shared writing in helping children to develop the confidence to explore possibilities through different language choices when writing independently?
- Does guided writing offer the perfect vehicle for deliberate practice?
- Does ACE IT! offer you a simple way of planning for, and assessing, writing that requires deeper thinking?
- How can we ensure that children get plenty of opportunities to practise their writing skills in English and across the curriculum?

6
Sequence

The **feedback** we give to guide children's efforts as they work through a **skills** journey in English, the ways we hook children into their learning through **talk and thought** and other means of **engagement**, and the **practice** children put in to improve are the principle threads to mastery learning in writing. We have considered each in some detail. Now we need to look at how we can draw these threads together to create effective sequences of learning in English.

F STEPS is only a useful checklist if it informs teachers' thinking as they sit down to plan a unit of work. Just like any successful golfer or tennis player has a routine to help them prepare for hitting the ball or serving effectively, teachers need to have some fundamentals in mind before medium-term planning. As we have already acknowledged, primary teachers are incredibly busy people these days with limited time to spend on planning. Yet, of course, the decisions taken by the teacher at this stage dictates the diet of learning that children receive. All the more reason to have a routine – a system for planning that helps to draw all the important threads together, and that becomes more comfortable and automated over time.

Figure 17 shows how all F STEPS strands are drawn together in the context of our planning pyramid to bring about an effective sequence of learning. The diagram shows the importance of practice, both in the development of oral language skills, through talk and thought, and in written language skills as children work towards particular outcomes. It also shows the central role played by feedback and engagement in inspiring and motivating children to produce their best.

In this chapter, we will reflect on these strands and consider how they fit into the different phases of learning in a unit of English work.

Overview of a unit of work

To organise a sequence of English lessons into consecutive phases, I would suggest three simple headings – Explore, Practise and Compose. This can be helpful both as a planning aid and to organise a working wall classroom display that captures the children's activity and supports their learning as they progress through the unit. Figure 18 shows some suggested activities teachers might want to consider in those three phases.

The Explore phase is very much about engagement. It involves exploring the meanings and themes behind texts and allowing the work of quality authors to inspire children's own thinking and writing. This phase is the home of talk and thought techniques like Exploratory talk and drama, and is our opportunity to ensure the learning context touches the children's lives in some way.

The Practise phase is where children take their thinking from the Explore phase, and explicit skills instruction from their teacher, into oral and written Practise of language skills. Once children begin to use skills themselves in their talk and in their writing, Feedback becomes a crucial part of the process. They

Figure 17 The complete F STEPS planning pyramid

Explore	Practise	Compose
Hook Reading as a reader Comprehension Text marking Drama Exploratory talk Philosophy for children Reading as a writer Free writing	Explicit teaching Oral activity Written activity Reasoning about skill Shared writing Drafting in context Helicoptering Editing/redrafting	Planning WAGOLL Shared writing Drafting Helicoptering Editing/redrafting

Figure 18 Suggested activities in a unit of planning across three phases

are already beginning to write in context when the sequence enters the Compose phase, where planning, further feedback through formative dialogue around progress and evaluation helps children towards what we will call 'destination' pieces of writing – the best texts children are capable of producing at the end of a unit.

The planning pyramid

We have established that the age-related grammar expectations for each year group, together with the skills that underpin them (identified in the Steps in Learning documents – Appendix 2), should be the main driver for a unit of work. Together with spelling, handwriting and composition objectives, these are the means by which children's writing is assessed and, if they are not used as the main driver, we risk learning being organised for children in an illogical order. Therefore, the teacher must first use assessment data to inform a decision about where the majority of childen in her class are up to in the Steps in Learning skills progression.

Let's say a Year 3 teacher decides that the majority of children in her class are getting the hang of writing two-clause sentences beginning with a main clause (e.g. Maddy went to bed after brushing her teeth.). She might decide that the next step for her class is to begin to write two-clause sentences beginning with a subordinate clause (e.g. Even though he wasn't very hungry, Colin ate all of his pasta.). There are a variety of factors that might come into play when choosing an appropriate text: pitch, interest, curriculum links, and so on. Having established the learning need, however, the teacher's priority must be to 'shop around' for a text that exemplifies the chosen skill in context.

An English unit of work might not be based on a text. We established in Chapter 4 that children's experiences, content from topic work and a range of other stimuli can provide the vehicle for children's learning. However, to cater for the demands of the National Curriculum, and to show good authors using skills in context, let us assume that some form of literature will provide this vehicle in most units of work.

Once a suitable text is identified, the teacher's thoughts need to widen to establish how that text can best be used to enhance the children's learning in that particular unit. This is where the teacher needs a simple, user-friendly routine for planning that they can employ again and again, trusting that it will help them deliver deeper learning in writing. Figure 19 is a simple model that will provide this routine.

Trying to focus on too much when beginning to plan sequences of learning in English can make life very difficult: often you can't see the wood for the trees. Spending 15 minutes or so thinking about three key F STEPS strands – skills, talk and thought and writing outcomes – is a very powerful way to produce an effective unit plan. If we can first see how a writing outcome can fall out of the chosen text, how that outcome would be enhanced through use of the focus skill (e.g. a variety of two-clause sentences) and how talk and thought can help children discover the ideas they will use in their writing, the unit almost begins to plan itself.

Skills

Skills, as the main driver for planning, are at the top of the pyramid. We looked at skills in detail in Chapter 2, including how the Steps in Learning documents can be used to identify which skills will be

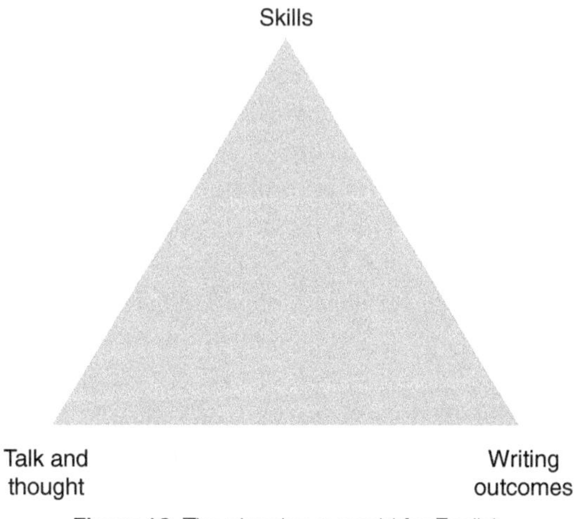

Figure 19 The planning pyramid for English

taught next. Seeing a good author using a particular skill well is the first chance children have of making sense of a new concept. Because it is used in a meaningful context, children not only gain knowledge of the concept but can see what effect it has on meaning.

Writing outcomes

Attention now needs to turn to the end of the process. What writing outcome do you want the children to produce at the end of the sequence? What is the destination writing outcome and what opportunity will there be for children to use and apply a newly-learnt skill? If we can establish what that outcome will be then we can plan backwards from that, deciding what children need in order to produce it. When going on a trip, we decide on the destination and plan the best route; we plan what we want in a garden before we landscape it. Starting with the end clearly in mind helps to ensure a successful outcome. The key for teachers is to choose a writing outcome that will be enhanced through use of the focus skill.

Talk and thought

Children need to engage with, and think deeply about, the context of their learning to discover the clear ideas they will need to produce the writing outcome. If we get the talk and thought right, through the use of Exploratory talk, drama or Philosophy for children, we can give children something to say and get them itching to say it. What better bridge to effective writing could we have?

Writing forms

Children need to have experience of writing in a range of different forms but we must remember that these forms are not dictated by the National Curriculum. Unlike the planning process we might have followed under the guidance of the Literacy Framework (2006), teachers should now feel free to ask children to write whatever they want them to write. So long as it is purposeful and provides children with an opportunity to create different effects in their writing by practising the skills they have been taught, any writing outcome is valid. Figure 20 shows how writing forms usually fall into one of three categories – entertainment, argument or persuasion. The forms of writing we have used traditionally in primary schools (shown in the upper part of the table) are still very important but it is also important to consider alternative forms of writing so that we don't limit the ways in which children can express themselves and apply their skills. The list of ideas shown is by no means exhaustive.

The choice of form for the destination writing will be informed by what the children have to say following their work in the Explore phase. The form needs to provide them with the best vehicle to say it. Whatever form is chosen, children will need to be clear about why their piece of writing exists. What is its purpose? Is it to entertain, inform or persuade? Junior children need to know that many texts can be multi-purpose. For example, a holiday or visitor brochure informs and persuades, a *Horrible Histories* book informs and entertains.

While considering which writing form gives children a meaningful opportunity to apply their skills, we should also consider how we might use the content of a text to get children to think. Does a main theme lend itself to enquiry through P4C or Exploratory talk? Is there an opportunity for children to get into role to explore an aspect of a story, such as characters' thoughts and feelings, or take it in an alternative

ENTERTAIN	INFORM	PERSUADE
STORY POETRY PLAYSCRIPTS	RECOUNT NON-CHRONOLOGICAL REPORT NEWS ARTICLE DIARY BIOGRAPHY EXPLANATION INSTRUCTIONS	ARGUMENT/ PERSUASION ADVERTISEMENT BALANCED DISCUSSION LETTER OF COMPLAINT
DESCRIPTION SONG COMIC STRIP	COMPARISON SUMMARY SPECULATION/ HYPOTHESIS (what if…?) PICTURE CAPTION	SPEECH EVALUATION (ranking/book reviews) ADVICE BLOG
LETTER, POEM, SONG, SPEECH…		

Figure 20 Range of writing forms

direction? If we can establish an opportunity for collaborative thinking then the form of the destination piece of writing will often present itself.

Teachers can use the pyramid to focus their minds on these important initial decisions when planning. In time, teachers will be brave enough to follow the children's lead in the Explore phase with regards to the writing outcome, and perhaps allow them to choose the form of writing for themselves. At least initially, though, they may prefer to choose the form of the writing outcome at the outset. In this way, they can influence the direction taken by the children's talk and be sure that the form and context of the writing presents children with a tailor-made opportunity to use and apply a new skill.

Ideas in practice

Name: Ashley Riley
Teaching level: Year 4
School: Moorfield Primary

I have worked with our English co-ordinator on planning using the skills/thinking together/writing outcome pyramid. We started with the Steps in Learning document for Year 4 and assessed the children's skills to identify the areas we wanted to target over the forthcoming half term. Our genres are set at the start of the year and this half term the focus was historical stories. We decided to focus on use of the perfect form of verbs. This led us into lots of thinking together through talk, including drama. The children interviewed each other and visitors in school as Roman characters from the text *Escape From Pompeii* by Christina Balit. This involved lots of 'Have you…?' questions answered with 'I have…'.

The character interviews were our first writing outcome but the character development that came from them fed into the writing of character descriptions as part of our historical stories. The talk sessions meant that the children were better prepared for writing. They gave the children chance to explore the characters in depth and build a bank of ideas and a wealth of vocabulary to use in their writing. The planning pyramid is a great starting point and having the greater focus on the Steps in Learning and the Exploratory talk definitely led to higher quality writing.

Things to think about

- What are the first decisions you make when you are beginning to plan a unit of work in English?
- Are your writing genres fixed in advance or are you free to use them in response to the needs of your children?

Long-term planning

One of the things we teachers get anxious about is coverage – including coverage of different genres and writing forms. This is understandable as planning ahead helps us to feel organised and we want to ensure that children experience a range of reading literature and writing styles. It is certainly important that we loosely map out where children will be exposed to different forms of fiction. I would simply urge teachers to allow the children's needs in terms of skills progression to dictate the teaching and learning, rather than allowing the teaching and learning of different forms to dictate the skills that the children are taught. This may just require a little more flexibility in our long-term plans. For instance, we could use the three fundamental purposes for writing – entertain, inform, compose – to ensure children have a balance of all three across a year and perhaps fuller coverage of all appropriate forms across an age phase. Specifically when each form is taught could then be left to the discretion of teachers so that they can respond to the needs of their class.

Planning using the pyramid, with the skills the class is ready for as the main driver, will not come naturally to many teachers to begin with. It may mean that planning grids stay blank for 15 minutes or so while a way to unite the three corners – skills, talk and thought and writing outcomes – becomes clear. It is well worth persevering, though. Once this is accomplished, the sequence of lessons for that particular unit should fall into place quite easily, and the reward is a meaningful flow of learning which incorporates four of the six strands of our F STEPS checklist: skills, talk and thought and engagement as part of an effective learning sequence.

The Explore phase

As we work backwards in our minds from the destination writing when planning, we consider the knowledge, understanding and experiences our pupils need to ensure their writing is as effective as possible. Before we can ask children to write in a context offered by a shared text, they need to be immersed in that context in ways already outlined. This may also involve hooking children into their learning, even before beginning to read, through a scenario, an artefact, a decorated classroom, a teacher in role, and so on.

It will certainly involve reading comprehension. As we share a new text, we want children to read for understanding and this requires their active participation – answering and asking pertinent questions. This I have referred to in Figure 18 as 'reading as a reader' and is a perfect opportunity for teachers to address the appropriate age-related expectations for reading. As we established in Chapter 2, one way of exploiting the synergy between reading and writing is to ask children for written responses to comprehension questions about a shared text. We need to recognise that these written responses are pieces of writing in their own right. In fact, extended written responses to questions like 'Why do you think Scrooge was so mean?' serve a number of purposes: they give children opportunities to practise their writing skills in a meaningful context, they can inform or be the outcome of class discussion, and they offer preparation for the sort of response-to-text writing that children are required to do in Key Stage 3 and 4.

Another important part of the Explore phase is 'reading as a writer'. This involves shining a spotlight on specific writing skills employed by an author: skills that you want pupils to recognise, understand and ultimately use in their own writing. If we look to these skills only after considering their effect on meaning and our reaction as readers then children's first introduction to elements of grammar is in the context of purposeful writing. This is an important opportunity for children to take what might be an abstract concept to them and make sense of it. A good way for children to demonstrate early understanding, recognising the focus skill independently, is through text marking.

Also, we should not underestimate the value of writing that is not intended for marking. Many people, including myself, prefer to think with a pen in hand and we should not deny children this opportunity to discover, record or develop their thoughts through writing. This can be very useful as an initial response to a text, or a question that falls out of a text. It can take place before oral dialogue, during oral dialogue or immediately after oral dialogue. In any case, it offers a guarantee of authentic writing. Perhaps our job as teachers is to channel and refine these initial ideas for a particular purpose. Steve Williams (2010) warns that denying learners these opportunities will make them too dependent on teachers to provide ready-made ideas, and that their own thoughts and intended meanings can get lost along the way.

The Practise phase

Having given children the opportunity to learn from a good author using particular skills well, a teacher needs to explicitly teach those skills before giving children time to practise them. This explicit teaching, which unpicks the focus skill and helps children understand the effect of language choices, begins the Practise phase. It may well involve consolidation of previous learning. In the above case study, the perfect form of verbs was taught to consolidate learning that took place when the concept was first introduced in Year 3. This would involve revision of other verb forms, such as simple past tense, and analysing the effect of using the verb *to have* as an auxiliary or 'helper' verb. Why would we choose to say or write 'We have played that game…' instead of 'We played that game…'?

Such teaching demands a response from children to see what they have understood. Ideally, this should be in the form of oral activity in which children can develop confidence with a new skill, learning from mistakes before committing their thinking to writing. Children can be very effective at evaluating each other's language use and the more the teacher can be aware of misconceptions and deal with them, at this oral stage, the better position children will be in to use language accurately in writing.

Some would argue that the next step should involve children applying their new knowledge and understanding in contextual writing. While I would not argue against this, I believe there are real benefits to asking children to initially practise the new skill out of context, using a simple prepared activity – at times as simple as dictating sentences incorporating the focus skill. This activity might take place in the same lesson as the oral rehearsal. It gives children the chance to focus attention on that skill in isolation and there is no risk of them producing writing without at least attempting to use the focus skill. It also gives the teacher a quick and easy opportunity to identify children who are struggling, deal with misconceptions and build confidence ahead of contextual writing.

This would be a means to an end, though – the end being application of the focus skill in context. It makes sense, then, that this contextual writing should happen very promptly after the non-contextual writing (perhaps the following lesson) but not before children have had the chance to talk – to reason – about the relevance of the focus skill. We discovered in Chapter 4 that children are more likely to remember and understand what they have learnt if they have an active role to play in figuring it out for themselves (discovery learning). When the teacher outlines a contextual writing task (designed as we have said to give children an opportunity to use and apply their new learning), he/she has the opportunity to get children to collaborate and work out why the skill they have just learnt will be useful for the task. Surely there is a much better chance of children using the skill appropriately if they have already made a connection between its purpose and the writing outcome.

Do all writing outcomes have to be lengthy? No, they don't. In fact, there is real value in shorter pieces of writing, particularly in English where the developmental work on particularly skills takes place. Shorter pieces of contextual writing are much more manageable for a child and can really help to focus his/her mind on a skill he/she is currently trying to develop. They are also much more suitable for comparison and analysis as part of group or class discussion.

This is the place in the sequence when serious consideration should be given to setting a shorter contextual writing task for children. Consider for a moment the thinking that a child needs to do to write a whole story. Depending on their age, they might need to think about how the story begins, create their character(s), perhaps include details about where their story takes place and what happens to their main character, who says what to whom, how to add atmosphere, and so on. This is all worthwhile thinking but if your main concern as a teacher is whether or not children can use and apply a newly-learnt skill, there is a good chance this will get lost as the children strive to move the story on.

We have reached a most important stage in the process, where children are ready to experiment with language in context. It is a great time for shared writing where the teacher can guide children's thinking and use of a growing repertoire of skills to pave the way for independent writing. This independent writing will be all the more effective if children's focus is narrowed. In the past, many teachers of English in primary schools have presented children with long lists of success criteria that they were expected to 'tick off' in a one-off piece of writing. This was overwhelming and stressful for children, and often focused their attention on features of a particular genre rather than their next steps as writers. An opportunity to try new skills, as well as work on their personal targets, in perhaps just a single paragraph informed by the rich dialogue of a shared write, is a completely different prospect for children.

This is not a destination piece of writing but a stepping stone towards that destination. For example, it may be a character description that will later be used in a story or it could be a paragraph in a non-chronological report, the lessons from which can be applied to other paragraphs in the final report. It is an interim piece of writing designed to develop children's confidence, not least because it presents the perfect opportunity for feedback and reflection. Teachers are in a position to give very precise support and challenge as children seek to put into practice all they have learned. On completion of the interim task, what better springboard for further learning do we have than using children's early attempts at writing in a particular context to prompt further discussion? The fact that these are short, focused pieces of writing means that this analysis can focus more easily and more precisely on particular language choices made by different children and their effect on meaning or impact for the reader.

Feedback and engagement

It is at this point, as children bring to their writing page all they have learnt from a particular author, from collaborative thinking with their peers and teacher, and from their shared writing, that children really make progress as writers – provided they have the right feedback. In Chapter 1, we explored in detail the crucial role played by feedback in motivating and refocusing effort as children are in the throws of deliberate practice. Children will engage with their personal targets if the challenge is right and teachers pay regular attention to whether they are improving or not. They will also become increasingly self-reflective if they are given clear guidance towards achieving their targets, and begin to drive their own learning forward. Rich formative dialogue at this stage in the process is crucial and can take the form of whole-class discussion, teacher-child conversations, child-to-child conversations and self-talk. The more children can learn from their early efforts of writing in a particular context, the more confident they will be about improving. Helicoptering offers a simple, child-friendly technique which embraces this range of dialogue and helps children to set clear intentions for their writing going forward.

The next writing task might be editing, and children need to be given a clear and simple system for annotating and making changes to their text. It may be re-drafting the interim piece of writing, or the teacher might choose to challenge children to write another interim text in a slightly different context – for example, another section of the non-chronological report that is the destination writing outcome. Either way, soon after the initial interim writing task, children need an opportunity to return to the lessons learnt from feedback dialogue and apply them through further writing.

Returning to our F STEPS checklist, we can see that all six of strands are now being drawn together in our sequence of learning. Figure 21 shows this in the context of our planning pyramid.

Not only have children been engaged in the sequence through the choice of text/stimuli and some form of collective thinking, they have also been engaged in their own progress as writers through dialogue, challenge and feedback. Children receive feedback as they practise both their oral use of language through collective thinking and their written use of language towards destination writing outcomes.

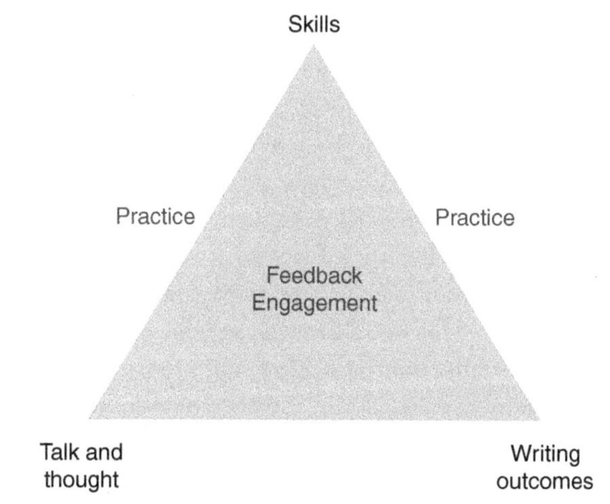

Figure 21 F STEPS delivered through the planning pyramid for English

The Compose phase

Clearly, children are already composing as they move into the Compose phase (Figure 20). Feedback – oral and written – is ongoing and should be prioritised because feedback, and children's reflection on it, is the biggest lever of progress. We talked in Chapter 1 about teachers working smartly in order to do just that, taking opportunities to save time elsewhere and using assessment data to target specific groups of children during the writing process. It is worth reiterating that feedback is at its most powerful when it refocuses effort towards specific goals and challenges children's thinking while they are writing. Teachers should work hard to maximise their impact during lessons and reduce the burden of less effective follow-up marking.

In the Compose phase, children's sights should be set on the destination piece of writing. They need to know what it could look like so that they can plan accordingly. Children's writing from a previous cohort can offer great model writing (WAGOLL) and so, too, can the product of shared writing. Of course, we don't want children to simply aspire to replicating this model writing. We want them to think creatively and bring their own interpretation to the set task. However, seeing a piece of writing deemed to be successful can help children to visualise what is expected of them. Better still, seeing examples of other writing deemed to be less successful will help them to evaluate the language choices made by the different children and make decisions about their own writing.

Also, if children are writing a newspaper article, they will need to see examples of newspaper articles. If children are writing a set of instructions, it is well worth them taking a look at recipes or instructions for a game. In this way, they become aware that these text forms have a function in the real world and they can begin to plan ahead for their own writing by becoming familiar with features, organisation and layout. We need to remember, though, that we don't need to get too anxious about children replicating genre features and organisation, and the reality is that children pick these things up very quickly. Ask yourself how long the children in your class actually need to get the idea of how to write a set of instructions and how long you have spent teaching instructional writing units in the past.

Planning for writing

Planning for writing is quite an abstract concept for children. Many fail to see the benefit of spending time preparing to write instead of simply getting on with writing, so they need to be shown both how to do it and why they should do it. Ideally, if the teacher occasionally did some writing alongside the children, he/she could share the thinking behind his/her planning. Alternatively, sharing the planning that preceded the above model writing can help children to see how the thinking done in advance of a writing task supported the writing process itself. They also need to know that it is ok to stray from plans as they change their minds or think of new ideas. After all, this is exactly what established authors do.

Planning might come in the form of notes under subheadings, a flow diagram or mind map. It is a way for children to gather their thoughts and ideas so that they can decide how they are going to tackle a piece of writing whilst calling to mind anything they particularly want to include. It is a statement of intent and should involve them thinking about how they might use particular skills they have practised in class and, crucially, how they intend to make progress against their personal targets. A plan is also a piece of writing in its own right and, as we have discussed, any piece of writing can be used a valuable springboard for further learning.

Having several children share their plans, explaining and justifying their thinking, is an excellent opportunity for those children to practise their speaking and listening skills. It also prompts class dialogue through questions, suggestions and comparisons. This is excellent preparation for writing and, in my experience, children relish the opportunity to return to their own plans afterwards to change, adapt and add new or borrowed ideas. This means a whole lesson devoted to planning but it is time spent very productively, allowing children to make sense of large amounts of information that came their way during the Explore phase, organise their thinking and begin to make language choices that will help them to say what they have to say.

There is another opportunity for shared writing here, before the children write their destination text. The collective thinking it offers around language choices, what works best and why, can help children to bridge the gap between their own ideas writing to their longer, grammatically elaborated pieces of writing.

Destination writing

The destination writing is important. It is the culmination of a lot of thinking and focused effort on the part of each child, and should be celebrated as such. We should never be tempted to teach the different phases of this sequence and simply end the process with individual pieces of interim writing. Children need to develop writing stamina by writing longer texts but, more importantly, they need the sense of achievement and satisfaction that comes from seeing the writing process through to its destination – a piece of writing that serves a purpose and can be read and enjoyed.

So who will read and enjoy their compositions? Could they act out their new scene of a play for another class, send their suggestions for the school field to the Chair of Governors, compare junior school to infant school for the soon-to-be Year 3 class or create a blog with their views on homelessness? As already discussed, there are also simpler things we can do routinely to ensure children have an audience beyond the teacher, such as reading their writing to a group or partner and regularly making books or magazines of children's work available to other children to read. However we do it, children will be more motivated to write, and can tailor their writing more precisely, if they are given a genuine audience for their writing.

Ideas in practice

Name: Sharon Houghton
Teaching level: Year 3
School: St Thomas of Canterbury

I used the planning pyramid to create a unit that linked our science topic on plants to English using a short film version of *The Giving Tree* by Shel Silverstein. I found the pyramid really useful to make sure the children did some deeper thinking and use this, along with newly-taught skills, to enhance their writing.

I started by bringing a bowl of fruit into class and we spent time talking about it – and eating it! We talked about the individual fruits, the colours, the differences and eventually the fact that they all came from a tree, they are good for you, etc. I showed the children the title picture of *The Giving Tree* and asked the children what they thought the film was about. I then used the film for comprehension. I wanted to focus on prediction and stopped the film at various points so that the children could discuss what they thought would happen next. They are getting used to backing up their ideas with reasons and asking their own questions about texts. One child asked why the tree in the story was a girl. This lesson ended with the children writing a prediction at the point of the story when the boy (or man by now) wanted a boat and the tree invited him to cut down her trunk to make one.

Next, I used the text to introduce prepositions, just as positioning words to begin with. We discussed the function of words like *in* and *from* before the children identified other prepositions in the first part of the text. I moved into the Practise phase here so that I could get the children to understand prepositions before a planned science lesson where they were gong to need them. So in English the children had a go at using prepositions orally – describing games they might play on the playground at lunchtime. We made a list of prepositions on the whiteboard that came up in these conversations. I then asked the children to write their own sentences in a different context, using words from the whiteboard.

In science, the children had already learnt about the different parts of a plant/tree. They drew a labelled diagram before writing a paragraph about the function of each part to the tree's survival. This was the children's first opportunity to use their knowledge of prepositions in context. I also used the opportunity to reinforce previous spelling working on creating plurals – roots, branches, leaves. In the next English lesson, we watched the whole of *The Giving Tree* film and did a P4C based on the question 'Are we a good friend to nature?'. The discussion was excellent. The children were quite clear that the boy in the story was not a good friend to nature, even though he began to regret what he did at the end. They were also able to talk about ways that we can be a good friend to nature, by doing things like looking after plants, planting new ones including ones that are friendly to bees, and feeding birds.

I later got the children to think in groups about how they might have ended the story differently if they were the author. Where would the story begin to change? What would happen? Could their science knowledge help them with their ideas? By now, the children had done more work in science on the life cycle of a flowering plant, including seed formation and dispersal. The children's ideas were amazing. One group had the original story running its course before the man brought his son back to the tree to show him where he used to play. They find a brand new apple tree growing close to the tree stump and make a promise to look after it and plant more trees at home to make up for the father's mistakes. Another group had the man stop short of chopping down the tree's trunk so that the tree could grow new branches, and launch a campaign to protect all the trees in the woods.

The children got more time to plan their alternative endings in mixed ability groups. Some of these plans were shared and this generated more discussion in which the children learned from each other. We also did some shared writing based on another idea of my own. The children wrote their stories over two sittings. We did lots of reflection after the first and the children were refocused on the use of prepositions and plural nouns, as well as their own writing targets. I look back on this as a really successful unit where everything came together to create quality writing.

Things to think about

- How can links be drawn between content in different subjects in your year group to deepen thinking and enhace writing?
- How often do your pupils get an element of choice in what they write?

This sequence is intended to help teachers get the best from their pupils. It is not a straightjacket. The activities suggested in Figure 20 are suggestions that can be expanded, contracted or omitted as appropriate to each unit. Some, though, are stakes in the ground around which effective units can be built: some form of collective thinking around a text or other stimulus, explicit skills teaching, shared writing and drafting with some form of reflection and subsequent editing or redrafting.

Reflection points

- Can you see the benefit of using the planning pyramid for English to help you design robust sequences of lessons aimed at delivering deeper learning for writing, focused on appropriate skills, collaborative thinking and purposeful writing outcomes?
- Do you use the freedom you have to plan for a wide range of writing outcomes that are purposeful and provide children with opportunities to practise the skills they have been taught?
- Could these include extended written responses to reading comprehension questions?
- Does splitting a sequence of learning in English into three phases – Explore, Practise and Compose – help you to visualise how a unit of work will roll out?
- Should the first phase of a unit (Explore phase) involve detailed exploration of a text and deeper thinking through some form of collaborative talk?
- Should the second phase of a unit (Practise phase) involve explicit teaching of new or reviewed skills followed by oral and written practise of those skills, shared writing and drafting in context, with opportunities to reflect and make improvements?
- Should the final phase of a unit (Compose phase) involve planning and writing at length, with opportunities to reflect and improve, as the culmination of a learning sequence?

Conclusion

We began with the premise that pretty much everyone can become an outstanding writer, and we have considered how we might create the right conditions in our schools and classrooms for this to happen.

Children's progress is at the heart of what we do as educators. The pursuit of it provides the challenge that accounts for endless hours of strategic ponderings as well as the rewards that keep us coming back for more. Achieving it is primarily down to the skills and mindset of the teacher – and the willingness and readiness of the children to learn. Today's teachers need to be ambitious for every child, have strong curriculum knowledge and an understanding of how best to use it. They need to be skilled at organising learning opportunities so that their pupils not only reach expectations but develop mastery of them by using and applying their learning across the curriculum. All this places great demands on teachers and it is vital that they feel fully supported in their efforts.

Unfortunately, as Developing Potential's 2015 research paper found, many of the initiatives schools embark upon to impact on progress are short term and not given sufficient time for benefits to come through. This can lead to schools lurching from one approach to the next as they look for the next best thing, without really stepping back to establish a clear long-term direction. It can also lead to frustration, demotivation and a lack of confidence among teachers.

Repeatedly shifting between strategies in pursuit of a long-term aim is counterproductive and does nothing for teacher wellbeing. Lots of teachers are anxious about workload and work-life balance. Having to respond to change again and again, whether they agree with it or not, will only exacerbate the problem. People's resourcefulness and performance decline as they experience anxiety or stress. As the Developing Potential report states:

> stressed teachers = stressed students;
> worried and anxious teachers = worried and anxious students;
> low-performing teachers = low-performing students.

This book acknowledges and salutes the hard work done by teachers, as well as the complexity and challenges of the job in the 21st century. It puts faith in high-quality research and encourages longer-term forward planning based on core strands of effective learning, such as practice, feedback and collaboration. School leaders need to build their development plans for English upon these fundamentally important strands and recognise that, like their pupils, teachers need time and support to hone their skills and practices before the rewards of their hard work can be reaped.

Developing growth mindsets, by building on what is working well and striving together for the next incremental improvements, is just as important for teachers as it is for pupils. To do this, I think school leaders have to keep the big picture in mind – a strong sense of purpose. What are we aiming for? In the context of this book, we are aiming for mastery learning in writing. Having a genuinely whole-school approach to achieving this aim is crucially important. Not an approach that stifles the creativity of individual teachers but one that creates buy-in from the whole team because they agree with the rationale behind it. One that develops the systems, routines and skills needed to get us where we want to be, and enables colleagues to work collaboratively on a shared vision.

School leaders must not only value outcomes or end results but also the process of bringing them about. Mastery learning is a process – a journey rather than a destination. If we can get children into the right learning habits in primary school, we can sow the seeds for a lifetime of successful learning in which they are intrinsically motivated to better themselves. The process offered by F STEPS is one in which teachers and children work together for sequential, goal-driven improvements, in which children think routinely, work collaboratively, practise their writing skills regularly and enjoy their learning journey.

F STEPS is not offered as yet another initiative but a refocusing on elements of the teacher's craft that will make the biggest difference to children's progress in writing. Turning it into a reality in school will take time and this need not be done all at once. Rather, it makes a lot of sense to prioritise those aspects that will make the biggest difference initially, as well as lay the foundations for further improvements, and then phase in other aspects – possibly over a period of several years.

Firstly, teachers' subject knowledge needs to be addressed. Many teachers, for instance, will not have been routinely taught grammar when they were at school. Schools need to be very clear on the **Skills** for writing they intend to teach their pupils (age-related expectations as well as the skills that underpin them) and ensure teachers understand not only the concepts themselves but how they can provide engaging learning opportunities for children to practise them. Secondly, a clear system for tracking children's progress against these skills needs to be put in place, as well as arrangements for target setting, feedback and interventions for those who need extra support.

Practice is at the heart of F STEPS – deliberate practice that focuses children's attention and efforts on skills just outside their comfort zone. The next priority for schools is to ensure teachers develop their skills in planning learning sequences that put skills development for purpose first, and provide opportunities for such practice. There should be a logical order to the skills journey in each year group (see Steps in Learning documents) and plans should include purposeful writing contexts across the curriculum. Precise **Feedback** is needed to continually channel efforts towards carefully-selected goals and, together with engaging learning experiences and writing opportunities, motivate children to take their next steps.

Engagement should be high on teachers' agendas when planning sequences of learning in English. Learning content and activities that are relevant to children's lives, or that capture their interest or imagination, get children wanting to write and are far more likely to generate authentic writing. Such engagement and authentic writing is all the more achievable if children are given regular opportunities to discover their own thinking through some form of enquiry-based talk: Exploratory talk, Philosophy for children or drama. Factoring such collaborative **Talk and thought** into learning sequences puts children's own ideas and experiences at the centre of their own learning and helps them to write from the heart. It may be the last piece of the jigsaw to be put in place.

When all said and done, the quality of teacher's planning will largely dictate the diet of learning that children receive. Investing time in supporting teachers to develop their skills in choosing appropriate texts and designing an effective **Sequence** of lessons is crucial to any school's subject development in English. This is a key role for English leaders. Planning English is not easy, particularly for less experienced or new-to-year-group teachers. All the more reason to establish a whole-school approach to planning that gives teachers a solid framework from which to start. A simple approach that is based on sound educational principles and, because of this, will stand the test of time and deliver results – both for teachers' confidence and expertise and for children's mastery of writing.

As a final thought, it is well worth considering how teachers in your school could be given opportunities to develop their own writing skills. Research completed by Teresa Cremin et al. (2017), alongside creative writing charity Arvon, and Teresa Grainger (2005), found real benefits to teachers writing alongside pupils at times, acting as role models and sharing struggles. Both projects urged teachers to experience writing for themselves in the safe, supported environment of the classroom because it allows them to learn about the complex process of writing from the inside out. Through becoming personally involved, thinking and feeling their way forwards as writers, they can gain insight into practices which help them develop both as teachers and as writers.

The National Writers Project is a network of teachers' writing groups, run by teachers for teachers. If you're interested in getting involved, visit www.nwp.org.uk.

Mike Cain can be contacted on: mdcain68@me.com.

Appendix 1
Helicopter task pro-forma

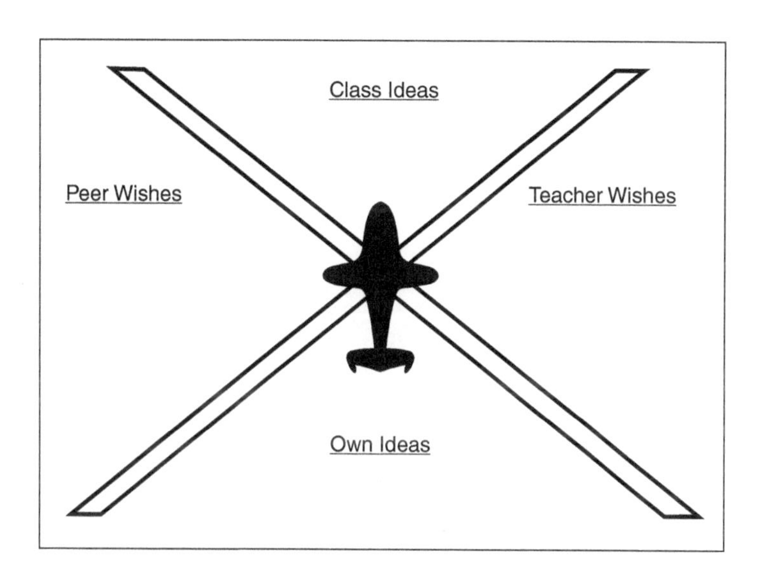

Appendix 2
Steps in Learning documents

Year 1

Year 1 writing – Steps in Learning					
Spelling	1	I can spell words that include the sounds I have been taught			
	2	I can spell my red words and days of the week (e.g. the, said, were, school)			
	3	I can name the letters of the alphabet in order and use letter names to say when the same sound is spelt differently			
	4	I can spell plural nouns and some verbs by adding -s or -es (e.g. cats/makes, bushes/catches)			
	5	I can use the prefix un- to change the meaning of words (e.g. unhappy, undo, unfair)			
	6	I can spell words ending in -ing, -ed, -er and -est (e.g. hunting, buzzed, quicker, freshest)			
	7	I can remember sentences my teacher reads to me and write them down correctly			
Handwriting	8	I can sit correctly at a table and hold a pencil comfortably and correctly			
	9	I am beginning to write my letters correctly			
	10	I can write capital letters and numbers 0-9			
	11	I know which letters to form in similar ways			
Composition	12	I understand what a sentence is and recognise sentences in my reading			
	13	I can say my sentences out loud			
	14	I can write sentences: sequencing them to form short narratives or recount events			
	15	I can write sentences: re-reading what I have written to check that it makes sense			
	16	I can discuss what I have written with the teacher or other pupils			

	17	I can leave spaces between words			
	18	I am beginning to punctuate sentences using a capital letter, full stop, question or exclamation mark			
		I recognise statements, questions and exclamations			
	19	I recognise nouns (singular and plural) as objects, people and places, and use them appropriately			
	20	I can use capital letters for names of people, places, days of the week and the personal pronoun **I**			
	21	I understand the job of an adjective and am beginning to use them to create simple noun phrases			
	22	I recognise verbs as action/doing words and use them appropriately			
		I recognise regular and irregular verbs (e.g. jump/jumped, take/took)			
		I can write in the past and the present tense			
	23	I can join words and clauses using **and**, **or**, **but**, **so**, **because**			

Grammar sequence

1 basic sentence punctuation (including statements, questions and exclamations)

2 nouns (including proper nouns)

3 noun phrases and pronouns to replace nouns

4 verbs, clauses and connecting clauses using conjunctions

Year 2

Year 2 writing – Steps in Learning					
Spelling	1	I can spell correctly by sounding out words			
	2	I can spell words including letter blends that sound the same but are spelt differently (including common homophones) (e.g. their/there, two/to/too)			
	3	I can spell my red words (e.g. because, behind, climb, every)			
	4	I can spell more contractions and words with the possessive apostrophe (e.g. can't/didn't/hasn't/I'll, Dad's hair/the girl's ball)			

	5	I know the difference between homophones and near homophones (e.g. here/hear, there/their/they're, one/won, quite/quiet)			
	6	I can add suffixes to spell longer words (e.g. -ment, -ness, -ful, -less, -ly, -tion)			
	7	I can remember sentences my teacher reads and write them down correctly			

Handwriting	8	I can write lower-case letters to the correct size			
	9	I can start using some of the diagonal and horizontal strokes needed to join letters			
	10	I can write capital letters (and numbers) correctly, making sure they are clearly bigger than my lower case letters			
	11	I can leave spaces between my words			

Composition	12	I am developing a positive attitude towards writing			
	13	I am developing stamina for writing by: writing about my own experiences (real and fiction); writing about real events; writing poems; and writing for different purposes			
	14	I can think carefully about what I am going to write by planning (writing down ideas/key words/new vocab) and talking about my ideas			
	15	I can make simple changes or add to my writing: after evaluating it with others; re-reading to check that it makes sense; proofreading for spelling, grammar and punctuation			
	16	I can begin to group ideas together in paragraphs			

Vocabulary, Grammar and Punctuation	17	I can use **1** full stops, **1** capital letters, **1** exclamation/question marks and **1** commas for lists correctly			
		1 I understand proper nouns and use capital letters appropriately (e.g. people, places, days, months)			
	18	**1** I can begin to use statements, questions, exclamations and commands (e.g. You are ready to go./Are you ready to go?/How incredible you are!/Get ready to go.)			
	19	**2** I can begin to use expanded noun phrases to describe and specify (e.g. a deep, dark cave/one cold night/the best night of his life)			
		2 I can choose nouns precisely (e.g. puppy instead of young dog)			
		I understand and use **1** nouns, **3** verbs and **2** adjectives			

		2 I recognise when adjectives do not improve my writing (e.g. The big dog ran along the flat path and jumped into the white snow.)			
		2 I recognise and use different pronouns (personal, subject, object, possessive) and use them appropriately			
	20	I can use suffixes to form **1** nouns, **2** adjectives and **4** adverbs (e.g. -ment/-ness, -ful/-less, -ly)			
	21	**3** I can begin to join clauses using a wider range of conjunctions (e.g. when, if, as, because, before, as well as, or, and, but, so)			
		3 I recognise verbs as doing words and being words (e.g. is, are, am, was, were)			
		3 I recognise a clause as an idea (e.g The spotty dog dug a hole.)			
	22	**3** I can begin to use present/past tenses correctly and consistently (including the progressive form) (e.g. I sit/I am sitting, I sat/I was sitting)			
		3 I recognise regular and irregular verbs (e.g. jump/jumped, take/took)			
	23	**4** I can begin to follow rules of Standard English (subject-verb agreement, consistency of tense)			
	24	I am beginning to use **5** inverted commas and **5** the apostrophe for contraction and possession (singular) appropriately			
		5 I am beginning to use apostrophes for contraction and possession (singular) appropriately (e.g. I will = I'll, the pen's lid)			
		5 I understand when <u>not</u> to use an apostrophe (e.g. verbs – gives/sings – and plurals – houses/friends)			

Grammar sequence

1 nouns (including proper nouns) and basic sentence punctuation (including statements, questions, exclamations and commands)

2 noun phrases and pronouns to replace nouns and noun phrases

3 verbs, clauses and connecting clauses using conjunctions

simple and progressive verb tenses

4 rules of Standard English and the introduction of adverbs

5 apostrophes (including when not to use them) and the use of inverted commas

Year 3

Year 3 writing – Steps in Learning					
Spelling		I know my key words and can spell most of the words on the Y3/Y4 spelling list			
	1	I can use further prefixes and suffixes and understand how to add them to root words (e.g. dis-/mis-/re-, -ly)			
	2	I can spell further homophones (e.g. here/hear, bury/berry, mist/missed)			
	3	I can spell words that are often misspelt from words taught so far (e.g. careful, parents, neighbour, disappoint)			
	4	I can use the first two or three letters of a word to check its spelling in a dictionary			
	5	I can write from memory simple sentences including words and punctuation taught so far			
H	6	I can use the diagonal and horizontal strokes that are needed to join letters			
	7	I can improve the quality of my handwriting (e.g. downstrokes parallel)			
Composition	8	I can plan to use the correct structure in my writing			
		I can open and/or end writing appropriately			
	9	I can use a wider vocabulary and grammar when I write			
		I can recognise and use similes (e.g. It was as fragile as a spider's web.)			
	10	I can organise paragraphs around a theme (e.g. build-up, main events, resolution)			
	11	I can create settings, characters and plot in stories			
	12	I can write non-fiction, using simple devices to organise my work (e.g. headings and subheadings)			
	13	I can evaluate and edit, learning from the effectiveness of my own and others' writing and making improvements			
	14	I can evaluate and edit, improving my writing by making changes to grammar and vocabulary			
	15	I can proofread for spelling and punctuation			
	16	I recognise and use the determiners **a**, **an** and **the** appropriately			

		I understand and use **1** nouns, **2** verbs, **1** adjectives, and **1** pronouns appropriately			
	17	**1** I can recognise and use words from the same word families, and use prefixes and suffixes to change the word class (e.g. unhappy, happy, happiness)			
		1 I understand which nouns can be proper nouns and use capital letters appropriately (people, places, days, months, titles, brands and some special occasions)			
		1 I understand statements (tell), questions (ask), exclamations (strong emotion) and commands (instruct) and use them appropriately			
		1 I can use a wide range of punctuation accurately and consistently (e.g. question marks, exclamation marks, commas in lists)			
		1 I can use expanded noun phrases to describe and specify (e.g. a deep, dark cave/one cold night/the best night of his life)			
	18	**2** I can use a wider range of conjunctions (e.g. since, even though, until) to extend a range of sentences with more than one clause			
		2 I can use commas to mark clauses (e.g. When we arrived, it was nearly midnight.)			
	19	**2** I can begin to identify main and subordinate clauses (e.g. Maddy went to bed after brushing her teeth.)			
	20	**2** I can use the perfect form of verbs (e.g. I have seen that film before.)			
		2 I recognise and use different verb tenses: simple past and present, past and present progressive			
	21	**3** I can use the apostrophe for omission and possession (singular and regular plural nouns) (e.g. the girl's game/the boys' dormitory)			
		3 I know and follow the rules of Standard English (subject-verb agreement, consistency of tense, avoidance of slang)			
		3 I understand when not to use an apostrophe (e.g. verbs – gives/sings – and plurals – houses/friends)			
	22	**3** I can use inverted commas to punctuate direct speech (e.g. "Don't be home late," called Mum.)			
	23	**4** I can recognise and use adverbs and prepositions (e.g. nervously/carefully, on/under/before)			
		4 I understand that some words belong to more than one word class (e.g. play, orange, swim)			

Grammar sequence

1 nouns (including proper nouns) and basic sentence punctuation (including statements, questions, exclamations and commands)

noun phrases and pronouns to replace nouns and noun phrases

2 verbs, clauses and connecting clauses using conjunctions

revision of simple and progressive verb tenses, and the present perfect tense

3 rules of Standard English

apostrophes (including when not to use them) and the use of inverted commas

4 using adverbs and prepositions (and recognising that words can belong to more than one word class)

Year 4

Year 4 writing – Steps in Learning					
Spelling		I can follow the Y3 spelling rules and spell most of the words on the Y3/4 word list			
	1	I can use further prefixes and suffixes and understand how to add them (e.g. il-, im-, -ir/-ous, -tion)			
	2	I can spell further homophones (e.g. threw/through, meet/meat, wait/weight)			
	3	I can spell words that are often misspelt from the Y3/4 word list (e.g. separate, library, to/two/too, a lot, their/there)			
	4	I can use the first two or three letters of a word to check its spelling in a dictionary			
	5	I can write from memory simple sentences including words and punctuation taught so far			

H	6	I understand which letters are best left unjoined (e.g. capital letters to any other letter, z)			
	7	I can improve the quality of my handwriting (e.g. letters consistent in size, ascenders and descenders not touching)			

Composition	8	I can plan to use the correct structure in my writing, adapting form and style			
		I can open and/or end writing appropriately			
	9	I can use increasingly varied vocabulary and grammar			

		I can use a variety of stylistic features for purpose and effect (e.g. alliteration, simile, metaphors, personification)			
		I can use techniques to engage the reader (e.g. build tension, opinion, rhetorical questions)			
	10	I can organise paragraphs around a theme, linking them when appropriate (e.g. topic sentences)			
		I can change paragraph with increasing accuracy (e.g. 3 Ps (person/place/point) and a T (time))			
	11	I can create settings, characters and plot in stories			
	12	I can write non-fiction, using simple devices to organise my work (e.g. headings and subheadings, bullet points)			
	13	I can evaluate and edit, learning from the effectiveness of my own and others' writing and making improvements			
	14	I can evaluate and edit, improving my writing by making changes to grammar and vocabulary			
	15	I can proofread for spelling and punctuation			
	16	I can read my own writing to a group or class using appropriate intonation/tone/volume so that the meaning is clear			

Vocabulary, Grammar and Punctuation		I understand, and use, **1** nouns, **2** verbs, **1** adjectives, **1** pronouns, **2** conjunctions, **4** adverbs and **4** prepositions appropriately			
	17	**1** I can choose nouns or pronouns to make my meaning clear and avoid repetition (e.g. Sam unwrapped his snack and picked up the bug. It tasted great!)			
		1 I can recognise and use collective nouns appropriately (e.g. swarm of bees, flight of stairs)			
		1 I can use the determiners **a**, **an** and **the** appropriately (e.g. a crazy idea, an iceberg, the sun) and recognise numbers as determiners			
		1 I can use a wide range of punctuation accurately and consistently (e.g. question marks, exclamation marks, commas in lists, inverted commas)			
	18	**2** I can use a wider range of conjunctions to extend a range of sentences with more than one clause			
		2 I can identify main and subordinate clauses accurately and consistently (e.g. It had been a fantastic day even though we got wet through.)			
		2 I can use powerful verbs to describe (e.g. the man collapsed instead of the man fell suddenly)			

		2 I can make the appropriate tense choices for a task (e.g. simple past, past progressive, present perfect for narrative)			
		3 I know and follow the rules of Standard English (subject-verb agreement, consistency of tense, avoidance of slang, avoidance of double negatives)			
	19	**3** I can use the apostrophe for contraction and possession (including regular and irregular plural nouns) (e.g. Jessica's book/the children's hobby)			
	20	**3** I can punctuate direct speech using inverted commas and other punctuation (e.g. comma after the reporting clause, end punctuation within inverted commas)			
	21	**4** I can use fronted adverbials followed by commas (range of sub sentences) (e.g. Later that day,… (when)/At the end of the road,… (where)/ Cautiously,… (how) + general)			
	22	**4** I recognise the difference between a clause and a phrase and use both appropriately (e.g. At midnight,… /When the clock struck midnight,…)			
	23	**4** I can use conjunctions, adverbs or prepositions to express time, place and cause (e.g. I'd never been before. (a)/She ate before she went out. (c)/He washed before tea. (p))			
		4 I can use expanded noun phrases with modifying adjectives and prepositional phrases (e.g. … in an isolated cottage at the top of the hill.)			

Grammar sequence

1 nouns (including proper nouns) and basic sentence punctuation (including statements, questions, exclamations and commands)

noun phrases and pronouns to replace nouns and noun phrases

2 verbs, clauses and connecting clauses using conjunctions

revision of verb tenses – simple, progressive and present perfect

3 rules of Standard English

apostrophes and direct speech punctuation

4 adverbs, adverbials and fronted adverbials (including the difference between a phrase and a clause)

using conjunctions, adverbs or prepositions to express time, place and cause

Year 5

Year 5 writing – Steps in Learning					
Spelling		I can spell most of the words on the Y5/Y6 word list			
	1	I can use further prefixes and suffixes and understand how to add them (e.g. -ous, -tion/-sion/-cian/-ssion, -able/-ible, -ably/-ibly)			
	2	I can spell some words with silent letters (e.g. island, doubt, knight)			
	3	I continue to understand the difference between homophones and other words often confused			
	4	I can use the first 3 or 4 letters of a word to check spelling or meaning (or both) in a dictionary			
	5	I can use a thesaurus for alternative word choices			

H	6	I can write legibly, fluently and with increasing speed			
	7	I can choose to write in pen or pencil, depending on the task			

Composition	8	I can plan my writing by: identifying the audience and purpose, selecting the appropriate form and using example texts to help me			
	9	I can plan my writing by: noting down my ideas from reading (and sometimes research)			
	10	I can draft and write by: choosing appropriate grammar and vocabulary for meaning and impact			
		I can use a variety of stylistic features for purpose and effect (e.g. alliteration, simile, metaphors, personification)			
	11	I can draft and write by: using a range of devices to develop my paragraphs in detail (e.g. adverbials, pronouns, conjunctions)			
		I can draft and write by: using a variety of techniques to engage the reader (e.g. build tension, comment, opinion, rhetorical questions, reflection)			
	12	I can draft and write by: describing settings, characters and atmosphere, and using dialogue to convey character and advance the action			

		I can draft and write by: establishing and maintaining a clear purpose and choosing content effectively to inform/engage the reader (e.g. link between opening and ending)			
		I can draft and write by: changing paragraph accurately and consistently (e.g. 3 Ps (person/place/point) and a T (time))			
		I can draft and write by: using other devices (e.g. headings, bullets, diagrams) to organise and present my writing and to guide the reader			
	13	I can evaluate and edit by: assessing the effectiveness of my own writing, including using a wider range of sentence structures for effect			
	14	I can evaluate and edit by: making changes to grammar, vocabulary and punctuation to improve impact			
	15	I can evaluate and edit by: using tense correctly throughout a piece of writing			
	16	I can evaluate and edit by: knowing the difference between the language of speech and writing			
	17	I can proofread for spelling and punctuation			

Vocabulary, Grammar and Punctuation		I understand, and use, **1** nouns, **2** verbs, **1** adjectives, **1** pronouns, **2** conjunctions, **2** adverbs, **2** prepositions and **1** determiners			
		1 I can use a wide range of punctuation accurately and consistently (e.g. question marks, exclamation marks, apostrophes, commas)			
		1 I can recognise and use abstract nouns (e.g. pain, laughter)			
	18	**1** I can use expanded noun phrases to give complicated information concisely (e.g. the dark green door with crumbling bricks on either side)			
		2 I recognise main and subordinate clauses, and phrases, and can use them to construct sentences in different ways			
	19	**2** I can use commas to make my meaning clear (e.g. Before leaving, the children said their goodbyes.)			
	20	**3** I can use the perfect form of verbs to show time and cause (e.g. Jason was tired because he had been jogging.)			
		3 I can make the appropriate tense choices for a task (e.g. simple past, past progressive)			
	21	**3** I can use modal verbs or adverbs to show how possible something is (e.g. may/could, nearly/definitely/always)			

		4 I know and follow the rules of Standard English (subject-verb agreement, consistency of tense, avoidance of slang, avoidance of double negatives, avoidance of adjectives as adverbs)			
		4 I can use direct and reported speech accurately (e.g. The teacher explained what they had to do.)			
		4 I can use colons to introduce a list (e.g. There were all sorts of animals there: pigs, goats, cows and chickens.)			
		4 I can use suffixes to convert from one word class to another (e.g. -ate, -ise, -ify/-ness, -ment/-ful, -ous)			
	22	**5** I can begin clauses with who, which, where etc or with an implied relative pronoun (e.g. Stanley arrived at the house, which stood at the top of a hill.)			
	23	**5** I can use brackets or commas to indicate parenthesis (e.g. The rose, which hadn't been watered, soon withered./Bob (our new coach) loves garlic.)			

Grammar sequence

1 nouns (including proper nouns) and revision of basic sentence punctuation (including statements, questions, exclamations and commands)

noun phrases and pronouns to replace nouns and noun phrases

2 verbs, clauses and phrases

using conjunctions and commas to connect clauses and phrases

3 verb tenses – simple, progressive and perfect

modal verbs and adverbs of possibility

rules of Standard English

4 direct and reported speech and suffixes to change word class

5 using relative clauses, and commas or brackets for parenthesis

Year 6

Year 6 writing – Steps in Learning					
Spelling		I can spell the words on the Y5/Y6 word list			
	1	I can use further prefixes and suffixes and understand how to add them (e.g. -fer, -ant/-ance/-ancy, -ent/-ence/-ency, -cious/-tious)			

	2	I understand the difference between homophones and other words often confused (e.g. principal/principle, stationary/stationery)			
	3	I can use my spelling rules when I write and understand that some words need to be learnt specifically			
	4	I can use dictionaries to check the spelling and meaning of words, and a thesaurus for alternative word choices			

H	5	I can write legibly, fluently and with increasing speed			

Composition	6	I can plan my writing by: identifying the audience and purpose, selecting the appropriate form and using example texts to help me			
	7	I can plan my writing by: noting and developing initial ideas, using reading and research when necessary			
	8	I can plan my writing by: thinking about how authors have developed characters and settings			
	9	I can draft and write by: selecting appropriate grammar and vocabulary, understanding how my choices change and enhance meaning			
		I can use a variety of stylistic features for purpose and effect (e.g. alliteration, metaphors, personification, puns, emotive phrases)			
	10	I can draft and write by: describing settings, characters and atmosphere and using dialogue to convey character and move the action on			
		I can draft and write by: using a variety of techniques to engage the reader (e.g. build tension, comment, opinion, reflection, expansion of key events, detailed characterisation)			
	11	I can draft and write by: summarising longer passages			
		I can draft and write by: establishing and maintaining a clear purpose and choosing content effectively to inform/engage the reader (e.g. link between opening and ending)			
		I can draft and write by: changing paragraph accurately and consistently (e.g. 3 Ps (person/place/point) and a T (time))			
	12	I can draft and write by: using a wide range of devices to make links within and across paragraphs (e.g. adverbials, conjunctions, pronouns, chains of reference)			
	13	I can draft and write by: using features such as subheadings and bullet points to structure text and guide the reader			

	14	I can evaluate and edit by: assessing the effectiveness of my own and others' writing			
	15	I can evaluate and edit by: proofreading and making changes to vocabulary, grammar, punctuation and spelling for effect and meaning			
	16	I can evaluate and edit by: knowing the difference between the language of speech and writing and using correct subject-verb agreement			
	17	I can perform my own compositions using appropriate intonation, volume and movement so that meaning is clear			
	18	I can sustain a convincing viewpoint throughout a piece of writing (e.g. authoritative or expert view/opinion)			

Vocabulary, Grammar and Punctuation		I understand, and use, **1** nouns, **2** verbs, **1** adjectives, **1** pronouns, **2** conjunctions, **2** adverbs, **2** prepositions and **1** determiners			
		1 I can use a wide range of punctuation accurately and consistently (e.g. question marks, exclamation marks, apostrophes, commas, brackets)			
		1 I can use suffixes to convert from one word class to another (e.g. -ate, -ise, -ify/-ness, -ment/-ful, -ous)			
		1 I can use expanded noun phrases to give complicated information concisely (e.g. the dark green door with crumbling bricks on either side)			
		2 I recognise main and subordinate clauses, and phrases, and can use them to construct sentences in different ways			
		3 I can use a range of verb forms (including the perfect form) to develop meaning and maintain appropriate tense choices			
		3 I can use modal verbs or adverbs to show how possible something is (e.g. may/could, nearly/definitely/always)			
		3 I know and follow the rules of Standard English (subject-verb agreement, consistency of tense, avoidance of slang, avoidance of double negatives, avoidance of adjectives as adverbs)			
	19	**3** I can use passive verbs in a sentence (e.g. The flag was raised by the dark knight.)			
		4 I can use direct and reported speech accurately and consistently (e.g. The teacher explained what they had to do.)			
	20	**5** I can use hyphens to avoid confusion (e.g. The best-dressed dancers win a special award.)			
	21	**5** I can use semicolons, colons or dashes between clauses and a colon to introduce a list			

	22	**5** I can use ellipsis (e.g. "I'm not sure what to …," he stammered./I love tea but [I] hate coffee.)			
	23	**5** I can recognise vocabulary & structures appropriate for formal writing (including subjunctive) (e.g. Furthermore,…/The doctor recommended he give up smoking.)			

Grammar sequence

1 nouns (including proper nouns) and revision of basic sentence punctuation (including statements, questions, exclamations and commands)

noun phrases and pronouns to replace nouns and noun phrases

2 verbs, clauses and phrases

using conjunctions and commas to connect clauses and phrases (including relative clauses and parenthesis)

3 verb tenses – simple, progressive and perfect

modal verbs and adverbs of possibility

rules of Standard English

using active and passive voice

4 direct and reported speech

5 using advanced punctuation (including colons, semicolons and dashes)

using vocabulary and structures for formal writing (including subjunctive form)

Appendix 3
Key words and prompts using Bloom's taxonomy

Questions for the Revised Bloom's Taxonomy

LEVEL 4 – ANALYSING		**LEVEL 5 – EVALUATING**		**LEVEL 6 – CREATING**	
Examine and break evidence into parts by identifying motives or causes. Make inferences and find evidence to support generalisations.		Present and defend opinions by making judgements about information, validity of ideas or quality of work based on a set of criteria.		Compile information together in a different way by combining elements in a new pattern or proposing alternative solutions.	
key words	**questions**	**key words**	**questions**	**key words**	**questions**
analyse categorise compare conclusion contrast discover distinguish divide examine function inference inspect list motive relationships simplify survey take part in test for theme	What are the parts of…? How is… related to…? Why do you think…? What is the theme…? What motive is there…? Can you list the parts…? What inference can you make…? What conclusion can you draw…? How would you classify…? How would you categorise…?	agree assess award choose compare conclude criteria criticise decide defend disprove dispute estimate evaluate explain importance judge justify opinion	Do you agree with the actions… / outcome…? What is your opinion of…? How would you prove/ disprove…? Assess the value/ importance of… Would it be better if…? Why did they (the character) choose…? What would you recommend…? How would you rate the…? How would you defend the actions…?	adapt build change choose combine compile compose construct create design develop discuss elaborate formulate happen imagine improve invent make up maximise minimise	What changes would you make to…? How would you improve…? What would happen if…? Can you elaborate on the reason…? Can you propose an alternative…? Can you invent…? How would you adapt… to create a different…? How could you change (modify) the plot (plan)…? What could be done to minimise/ maximise…?

key words	questions	key words	questions	key words	questions
	Can you identify…? What evidence can you find…? What is the relationship between…? Can you distinguish between…? What is the function of…? How can you justify…?	prioritise prove rate recommend select support value	What choices…? How would you prioritise…? What judgement can you make…? Based on what you know, how would you explain…? What information would you use to support the view…? How would you justify…? Why was it better that…? How would you compare the… ideas (people)?	modify original plan predict propose solution solve suppose test theory	How would you design…? What could be combined to improve (change)…? Suppose you could… What would you do…? How would you test…? Can you formulate a theory for…? Can you predict the outcome if…? Can you think of an original way for the…?

Bibliography

Andrews, R., Torgerson, C., Beverton, S., Freeman, A., Locke, T., Low, G., Robinson, A. and Zhu, D. (2006), 'The Effect of Grammar Teaching on Writing Development', *British Educational Research Journal*, 32(1), 39-55.

Barrs, M. and Cork, V. (2001), *The Reader in the Writer: The links between the study of literature and writing development at Key Stage 2*. London: CLPE.

Bearne, E., Grainger, T. and Wolstencroft, H. (2004), *Raising Boys' Achievements in Writing*, Leicester: The United Kingdom Literacy Association.

Berninger, V.W., Berninger, R. D., Abbott, S. P., Graham, S., Richards, T. (2002), 'Writing and Reading: Connections Between Language By Hand and Language By Eye', *Journal of Learning Disabilities*, 35(1), 39-56.

Black, P. and William, D. (1998), 'Assessment and Classroom Learning', *Assessment in Education: Principles, Policy & Practice*, 5(1), 7-74.

Bryant, J., Hezel, R. and Zillmann, D. (1979), 'Humor in children's educational television', *Communication Education*, 28(1), 49-59.

Bullock, A. (1975), *A Language for Life: Report of the Committee of Enquiry appointed by the Secretary of State for Education and Science*. London: Her Majesty's Stationery Office.

Butler, D.L. (1998), 'A Strategic Content Learning Approach to Promoting Self-Regulated Learning by Students With Learning Disabilities', in D.H. Schunk and B.J. Zimmerman (eds.), *Self-Regulated Learning: From Teaching to Self-Reflective Practice*. New York: Guilford.

Camby, S. (2015), *Mastery & Depth in the National Curriculum*. Saddleworth: Focus Education UK Ltd.

Clark, C. and Teravainen, A. (2017), *Celebrating Reading for Enjoyment: Findings from our Annual Literacy Survey 2016*. London: National Literacy Trust.

Clear, J. (2017), 'Lessons on Success and Deliberate Practice from Mozart, Picasso, and Kobe Bryant', available at: www.jamesclear.com/deliberate-practice

Corbett, P. (2015), 'Encourage Good Literacy Habits With These Shared Writing Activities', available at: https://www.teachwire.net/news/pie-corbett-encourage-good-literacy-habits-with-these-shared-writing-techni

Cremin, T. (2016) 'Writing for Pleasure?', available at: www.teachersaswriters.org/general/writing-for-pleasure/

Cremin, T., Goouch, K., Blakemore, L., Goff, E. and Macdonald, R. (2006), 'Connecting drama and writing: seizing the moment to write', *Research In Drama in Education*, 11(3), 273-291.

Cremin, T., Myhill, D., Eyres, I., Nash, T., Wilson, A. and Oliver, L. (2017), *Teachers as Writers*, Leicester: The United Kingdom Literacy Association.

Dawes, L., Littleton, K., Mercer, N., Wegerif, R. and Warwick, P. (date unknown), *Thinking Together in the Primary Classroom*. Milton Keynes: The Open University.

Dawes, L. and Sams, C. (2004), 'Developing the Capacity to Collaborate', in K. Littleton, D. Miell and D. Faulkner (eds.), *Learning to Collaborate: Collaborating to Learn*. Hauppauge: Nova Science Pub. Inc.

Developing Potential (2015), *Raising Attainment – A Whole School Approach to Improving Wellbeing, Building Resilience and Developing Growth Mindsets*.

The Department for Education and Skills (2006), *Primary Framework for literacy and mathematics*, available at: http://www.educationengland.org.uk/documents/pdfs/2006-primary-national-strategy.pdf

Dweck, C.S. (2000), *Self-theories: Their role in Motivation, Personality and Development*, Florence, KY: Psychology Press.

Education Endowment Foundation (2015), *Philosophy for Children: Evaluation report and Executive summary*, available at: v1.educationendowmentfoundation.org.uk/uploads/pdf/Philosophy_for_Children.pdf

Emmitt, M, Hornsby, D. and Wilson, L. (2013), *The Place of Phonics in Learning to Read and Write.* Adelaide: Australian Literacy Educators' Association.

Ericsson, A. and Pool, R. (2017), *Peak: How all of us can achieve extraordinary things.* London: Vintage.

eurostat: Your key to European statistics (2018), available at: http://ec.europa.eu/eurostat

Falk, B. (2012), *The Wonder of Brian Cox: The Unauthorised Biography of the Man Who Brought Science to the Nation.* London: John Blake Publishing Ltd.

Fisher, R. (date unknown), *Fostering Curriculum for Excellence Capacities: Thinking to learn – learning to think.* Inverness: The Highland Council.

Flavell, J.H. (1979). 'Metacognition and cognitive monitoring: A new area of cognitive–developmental inquiry', *American Psychologist*, 34(10), 906-911.

Flood, A. (2015), 'National curriculum is damaging children's creative writing, says authors'. *The Guardian*, available at: https://www.theguardian.com/books/2015/jun/23/national-curriculum-is-damaging-childrens-creative-writing-say-authors

Fry, E.B., Fountoukidis, D. and Polk, J.K. (1985), *The New Reading Teacher's Book of Lists.* Englewood Cliffs, NJ: Prentice-Hall.

Gardner, H. (1983), *Frames of Mind: The Theory of Multiple Intelligences.* New York: Basic Books.

Gawande, A. (2011), *The Checklist Manifesto: How to Get Things Right.* London: Profile Books Ltd.

Graham, S., Herbert, M. and Harris, K.R. (2015), 'Formative Assessment and Writing: A Meta-Analysis', *The Elementary School Journal,* 115(4).

Grainger, T. (2005), 'Teachers as writers: learning together', *English in Education*, 39(1), 75-87.

Hanna, P.R., Hanna, J.S., Hodges, R.E., Rudorf, E.H., United States Office of Education and Stanford University (1966), *Phoneme-Grapheme Correspondences as Cues to Spelling Improvement.* Washing, DC: U.S. Department of Health, Education and Welfare, Office of Education.

Hattie, J. and Jaeger, R. (1998), 'Assessment and Classroom Learning: a deductive approach', *Assessment in Education: Principles, Policy & Practice*, 5(1), 111-122.

Hattie, J. (2003), '*Teachers Make a Difference: What is the Research Evidence?',* available at: http://research.acer.edu.au/research_conference_2003/4/

Hattie, J. (2012), *Visible Learning for Teachers: Maximizing Impact on Learning.* Oxon: Routledge.

Heathcote, D. and Bolton, G. (1994), *Drama for Learning: Dorothy Heathcote's Mantle of the Expert Approach to Education.* Portsmouth, NH: Heinemann Press.

Hillocks, G. Jr. (1984), 'What Works in Teaching Composition: A Meta-Analysis of Experimental Treatment Studies', *American Journal of Education*, 93(1), 133-170.

Hornsby, D. and Wilson, L. (2011), *Teaching Phonics in Context.* Melbourne: Pearson Australia.

Jerrim, J. (2012), 'The socio-economic gradient in teenagers' literacy skills: how does England compare to other countries?', in *DoQSS Working Papers.* London: Department of Quantitative Social Science – UCL Institute of Education, University College London.

Kohn, A. (2004), 'Feel-Bad Education: The Cult of Rigor and the Loss of Joy', *Education Week*, available at: https://www.edweek.org/ew/articles/2004/09/15/03kohn.h24.html

Lipton, B.H. (2013), *The Honeymoon Effect: The Science of Creating Heaven on Earth.* London: Hay House UK Ltd.

Littleton, K. and Mercer, N. (2013), *Interthinking: Putting talk to work.* Oxon: Routledge.

Locke, E.A. and Latham, G.P. (1984), *Goal Setting: A Motivational Technique That Works.* Englewood Cliffs, NJ: Prentice-Hall.

Mercer, N. (2008), 'Developing Dialogues', in G. Wells and G. Claxton (eds.), *Learning for Life in the 21st Century: Sociocultural Perspectives on the Future of Education,* Oxford: Wiley-Blackwell.

Mercer, N. (2013), 'The Social Brain, Language and Goal-Directed Collective Thinking: A Social Conception of Cognition and its Implications for Understanding How We Think, Teach and Learn', *Educational Psychologist,* 48(3), 148-168

Myhill, D., Jones, M.D., Lines, H. and Watson, A. (2012), 'Re-thinking grammar: the impact of embedded grammar teaching on students' writing and students' metalinguistic understanding', *Research Papers in Education*, 27(2), 139-166.

Ofsted (2012), *Moving English Forward: Action to raise standards in English*, available at: www.ofsted.gov.uk/resources/moving-english-forward

Pawlak, R., Magarinos, A.M., Melchor, J., McEwen, B. and Strickland, S. (2003), 'Tissue Plasminogen Activator in the Amygdala is Critical for Stress-Induced Anxiety-Like Behavior', *Nature Neuroscience*, 6(2), 168-74.

Polanyi, M. (1967), The Tacit Dimension. London: Routledge & Keegan Paul.

The Reading Agency (2018), 'Reading Facts', available at: https://readingagency.org.uk/about/impact/002-reading-facts-1/

Robertson, C. (2015), 'The True Secret Behind Mozart's Genius', available at: http://www.willpowered.co/learn/true-secret-mozart

Rosen, M. (1998), *Did I Hear You Write?*. Nottingham: Five Leaves Publications.

Ryan, A.M., Pintrich, P.R. and Midgley, C. (2001), 'Avoiding Seeking Help in the Classroom: Who and Why?', *Educational Psychology Review*, 13(2), 93-114.

The Save the Children Fund (2014), *How Reading Can Help Children Escape Poverty*.

Scottish Book Trust (2018), 'Creating a Reading Culture: Get your whole school reading', available at: http://www.scottishbooktrust.com/learning/learning-resources/resource/creating-a-reading-culture-get-your-whole-school-reading

Slavin, R.E. (2009), *Educational Psychology: Theory and Practice*. London: Pearson.

Stambor, Z. (2006), 'How Laughing Leads to Learning', *Monitor on Psychology*, 37(6), 62.

Syed, M. (2011), *Bounce: The Myth of Talent and the Power of Practice*. London: 4th Estate.

Taylor, T. (2016), *A Beginner's Guide to Mantle of the Expert: A Transformative Approach to Education*. Norwich: Singular Publishing Limited.

Taylor, T. (2013), 'Why learning and having fun are not inimical', available at: http://www.imaginative-inquiry.co.uk/2013/10/why-learning-and-having-fun-is-not-inimical/

Taylor, T. and Edmiston, B. (date unknown), 'The Mountain Rescue Team', available at: www.mantleoftheexpert.com/wp-content/uploads/2018/01/Mountain-Rescue.pdf

Topping, K.J. and Trickey, S. (2007), 'collaborative philosophical inquiry for schoolchildren: Cognitive gains at 2-year follow-up', *British Journal of Educational Psychology*, 77(4), 787-796

Vass, E. and Littleton, K. (2010), 'Peer collaboration and learning in the classroom', in Littleton, K., Wood, C.and Kleine Staarman, J. (eds.), *International Handbook of Psychology in Education*. Leeds: Emerald.

Vygotsky, L.S. (1962). *Thought and Language*, Cambridge, MA: MIT Press.

Williams, S. (2010), 'Thinking With Concepts', in *Sapere Handbook* to accompany the Level 1 course (3rd Edition), Abingdon: Sapere.

Williams, S. (2008), 'Writing, Thinking and Dialogue', available at: www.p4c.com

Willis, J. (2007), 'The Neuroscience of Joyful Education', *Educational Leadership*, 64.

Winsor, P. and Pearson, P.D. (1992), *Children at Risk: Their Phonemic Awareness Development in Holistic Instruction*. Champaign: University of Illinois at Urbana-Champaign.

Wyse, D. (2004), 'Grammar. For Writing? A Critical Review of Empirical Evidence', *British Journal of Educational Studies*, 49(4), 411-427.